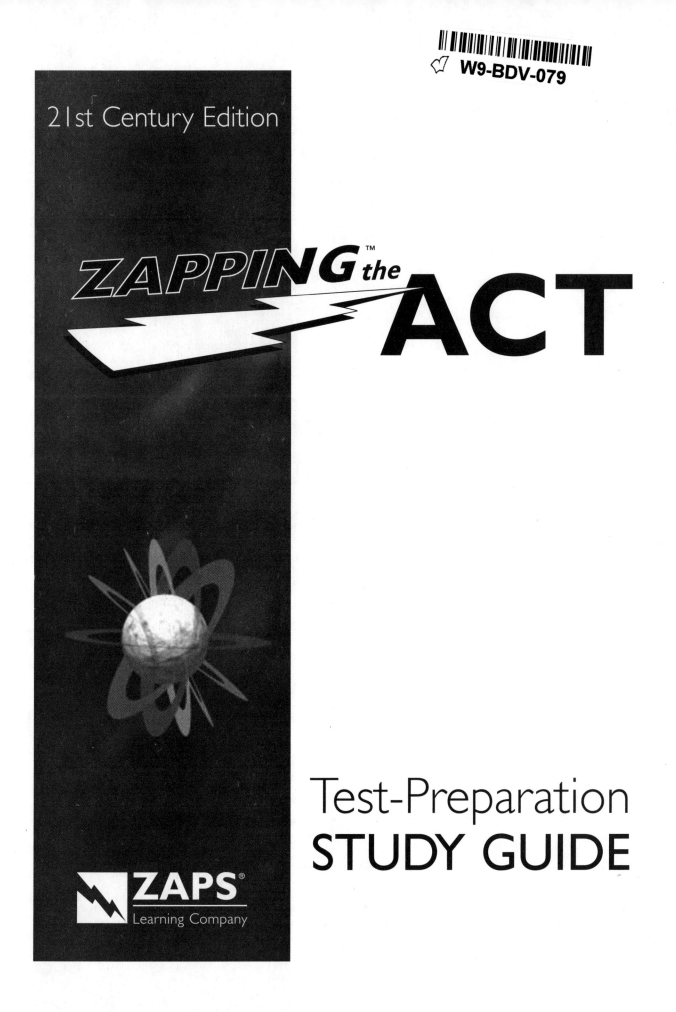

W9-BDV-079

21st Century Edition

ZAPPING the ACT™

Test-Preparation
STUDY GUIDE

ZAPS®
Learning Company

ISBN 0-7836-2397-6

4 5 6 7 8 9 10

Table of Contents

An Important Letter from ZAPS Learning Company

Dear Student,

The ACT is a fairly ordinary test that has acquired extraordinary powers. If you need to take it—either to get into college or to try for a scholarship—then you should do everything possible to prepare yourself. This is a competitive examination. You MUST be ready if you want to do your best.

Your ACT score is the average of your scores on four subject tests: English, Mathematics, Reading, and Science Reasoning. There is also an optional essay test. The best way to attack each section of the ACT depends on your personal abilities and natural test-taking habits. Many students raise their scores by slowing down. Others need to speed up. Some students get hung up on English, others on Mathematics or Science. Many students panic and turn the whole day into a miserable experience.

I want to help you. Depending on your ability level, you will score within a fairly predictable range on each subtest of the ACT. The goal of this program is to help you score at the top of your range.

Good luck on the test!

Sincerely,

Douglas J. Paul, Ph.D.
Founder

P.S. After you take the test, please visit our website and share any feedback that you might have about the experience. You can find us at: *www.zaps.com*

How to Use This Book

This Study Guide is divided into several sections:

1. Introduction and General Tips

2. English

3. Mathematics

4. Reading

5. Science Reasoning

6. Appendix A: Special pages for students participating in a workshop

7. Appendix B: Scoring information

8. Appendix C: Answer reviews for Training Workouts

Accompanying this Study Guide are 27 Training Workouts. Detailed answer explanations for all the Training Workouts are included in Appendix C. Below are a few tips to help you get the most out of these study materials.

1. **Begin preparing well in advance.** Don't wait until the night before the test.

2. **Set aside a few minutes every day to practice.** We recommend 30 minutes each day.

3. **Create a personalized study plan.** How you design your study plan will depend on the amount of time you have until the test and on your personal strengths and weaknesses in the four content areas. A suggested Kick-off Plan is given below.

Eight Step Kick-Off Plan

Step 1: Read the Introduction and take the one English Training Workout.

Step 2: Read the English tips and review answer explanations for the test you took on Day 1.

Step 3: Take one Math Training Workout.

Step 4: Review the math tips and answer explanations for the Math Test you took on Day 3.

Step 5: Review the reading tips and take one Reading Training Workout.

Step 6: Study the answer explanations for the Reading Test you took on Day 5.

Step 7: Review the science tips and take one Science Training Workout.

Step 8: Study the answer explanations for the Science Test you took on Day 7.

Suggestions for focusing your additional practice sessions are given in the "Using the Program on Your Own" tips at the beginning of each section of this Study Guide.

Introduction

What's on the Test?

Let's take a look . . . Open your copy of The ZAP–ACT English Training Workout.

THE ACT ENGLISH TEST
45 minutes   75 items

Tests your knowledge of written English:

- punctuation
- grammar
- sentence structure
} **Usage & Mechanics** (40 items in all)

- strategy
- organization
- style
} **Rhetorical Skills** (35 items in all)

The left column presents a passage—the right column presents questions.

For most of the questions, something is underlined in the passage; you need to choose the correct way to write each underlined part. As you read the passage, you will be considering the different choices. It looks harder than it is.

About two or three questions on each passage will be style, organization, or strategy items. For example, look at items 8 and 25. These items are indicated by a special box instead of by an underlined part of the sentence. To answer these type of problems, you need to read the test as if you were editing it.

Take a look at the ZAP-ACT Mathematics Training Workout.

THE ACT MATHEMATICS TEST
60 minutes   60 items

Tests your ability to solve regular math problems:

- arithmetic and pre-algebra   12 items
- elementary algebra   12 items
- intermediate algebra and coordinate geometry   18 items
- plane geometry   14 items
- trigonometry   4 items

The people at ACT have arranged the math problems in the order that *they* think is from easy to hard. However, when you take the test, you'll find the easy ones mixed in with the hard ones. On the ACT math test, algebra is mixed in with arithmetic and geometry.

If you have taken a regular series of math classes (pre-algebra, algebra I, geometry, algebra II), there shouldn't be more than three or four problems that seem totally over your head.

Take a look at the ZAP-ACT Reading Training Workout.

THE ACT READING TEST
35 minutes   40 items

Tests your ability to read and answer questions about the passage:

• identify supporting details

• draw conclusions

• make comparisons

• make generalizations

You will read four passages and answer ten questions on each passage. This test is not much different from all the other standardized reading tests you've taken.

Take a look at the ZAP-ACT Science Training Workout.

THE ACT SCIENCE REASONING TEST
35 minutes   40 items

This test has some of the features of a reading comprehension test, only with a science angle. Instead of a passage, you will read an "information set" and then answer questions. There are three types of information sets:

• research summaries (descriptions of experiments and results)

   3 passages with 6 items each

• data representation (charts with some descriptive text)

   3 passages with 5 items each

• conflicting viewpoints (reading comprehension, alternative hypotheses or views)

   1 passage with 7 items

THE ACT ESSAY TEST (OPTIONAL)

There is also an optional Essay Test. You are given a short prompt and you have to write about one page. No factual information is required.

Take Control of the ACT Competition

Think of this challenge as a competition. You do not need to let ACT control every aspect of this contest. The more YOU take control, the better chance you have at reaching your highest personal potential.

ACT CONTROLS—

1) date and location of the test

2) environment for administration

3) technical specifications of the test

4) sequence of item presentation

5) raw score (number correct) to ACT score conversion

These five elements are beyond your control. These are the "givens." There are other important elements, however, that you CAN control.

YOU CONTROL—

1) level and intensity of advance preparation

2) your personal scoring goals

3) attack strategy for each subtest

4) sequence of questions you choose to answer

5) mental attitude before and during the test

Do not surrender control of the factors you CAN control.

GOAL: To help you achieve your highest possible score on each subtest of the ACT.

Your personal "highest possible score" depends on your ability in each subject. When you take the ACT, there are a number of factors that can lower your score. The goal of test preparation is to minimize the effects of those negative factors.

OBJECTIVE 1: To demystify the ACT competition.

In order to get your highest possible score in the ACT competition, you need to know as much as possible about the test. In this Study Guide and in the accompanying tests, you will be presented with each type of question on the ACT, the difficulty levels you should expect, and the content you need to master in order to do well.

OBJECTIVE 2: To reduce test anxiety and its negative effects on your scores.

The ACT competition is guaranteed to create as much anxiety as possible. Although we can't change the testing situation, we can help you take control of it. These study materials will help you know what to expect so that you will find the situation more familiar. And when the test actually begins, your preparation will reduce overall anxiety. You will be less likely to panic during the test because you will have a variety of strategies to employ when you don't know the answer to a problem.

OBJECTIVE 3: To teach you both general and specific strategies for taking multiple-choice tests.

This Study Guide covers numerous strategies for taking tests. Some of these methods will become tools that you may apply to any multiple-choice test. Other strategies are specific to the types of items that appear on the ACT.

The emphasis of this book is on what to do when the correct answer to a problem is not immediately known. The main strategy, called *ZAPPING*, teaches you to identify and eliminate incorrect choices before selecting an answer. This strategy is modified slightly for each type of ACT item. *ZAPPING* is a technique you can transfer to every multiple-choice test that you take in high school or college.

OBJECTIVE 4: To provide an outline for approaching the optional essay test.

A Note About Timing

Like many competitive events, all of the ACT subtests are timed. Many students who have the skills necessary to eventually find all of the right answers do poorly only because of a timing problem.

Wear a watch to the test!

The first thing to do at the start of each session is to write down the time that it will end. The people who administer the test are instructed to announce when you have five minutes left. They are also free to write the start and stop time on the board. Don't count on them—they may fail to give you this courtesy. *And don't rely on your memory!*

Many of the test-taking strategies in this book will require you to be aware of the time all the way through the test, not just at the end. We have two recommendations on where to write the time. Take your pick:

• **Our favorite spot:** Write it on the front cover of your test book. If you write it somewhere in the middle of the test, you will have to flip to find it. Although you'll need to turn to the cover to see the time, at least you'll be able to do this quickly.

• **The worst choice:** Many students think they will simply remember the stop time. Don't try it. When you are concentrating on the test, it's very difficult to keep timing in mind. Write it down.

At the start of EVERY test, write down the time for completion. This is an easy place to establish control.

Guessing

NEVER, EVER, for any reason, leave any blanks on the ACT. Blind guessing cannot hurt you—
it can only help you.

If you leave blanks on this test, you are throwing away points.

Whenever possible, try to eliminate choices BEFORE you guess. By learning ways to eliminate
wrong choices, you can significantly increase your score.

ZAPPING

ZAPS Learning Company has developed a strategy for "zeroing-in" on the right answer before
picking. It's called *ZAPPING*. The exact method of *ZAPPING* is different for each type of
question on the ACT.

Zero-in And Pick

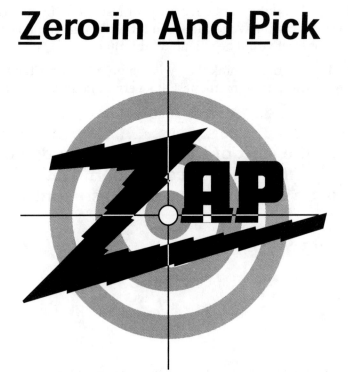

For all of the subtests on the ACT:

1) If you know the answer, answer the question.

2) If you don't know the answer, *ZAP* before you guess.

3) If you can't *ZAP*, then make a blind guess.

How Does *ZAPPING* Work?

The difficulty of multiple-choice tests is not controlled simply by the questions. It is also determined by the wrong answer choices. Three versions of a sample test question will illustrate this point.

Version One: Moderate to hard difficulty

Which president added a corollary to the Monroe Doctrine?
- **A.** William Henry Harrison
- **B.** William Howard Taft
- **C.** Theodore Roosevelt
- **D.** Woodrow Wilson

Version Two: Changed by an editor to make it easier

Which president added a corollary to the Monroe Doctrine?
- **A.** Ronald Reagan
- **B.** William J Clinton
- **C.** Theodore Roosevelt
- **D.** Ralph Nader

Notice that the question in Version Two is the same as Version One. The correct answer is also the same. The item is easier because more students will be able to eliminate the wrong choices.

Let's take a look at one more revision of this question. Again, notice that the question and correct answer remain the same.

Version Three: Easy

Which president added a corollary to the Monroe Doctrine?
- **A.** Celine Dion
- **B.** Homer Simpson
- **C.** Theodore Roosevelt
- **D.** Shaquille O'Neal

The point of Version Three is to demonstrate that even a difficult item becomes simple if the choices are ridiculous.

If you can learn ways to make wrong choices in the ACT more obvious, the questions will become easier—AND your scores will go up.

Part of your challenge when you take the ACT is to spot choices that are like Homer Simpson and Shaq.

Multiple-choice items are naturally vulnerable to *ZAPPING*. We can look at the writing and editorial effort as the process of putting test items together. In the same way, we can think of *ZAPPING* as taking test items apart.

Some students discover *ZAPPING* as naturally as learning to walk. If you have always *ZAPPED* multiple-choice tests, you are starting this program with a serious advantage. The focus now will be to learn specific *ZAPPING* strategies for each type of question used in the ACT competition.

It is not really possible to construct a machine-scorable multiple-choice test that is completely invulnerable to *ZAPPING*. Besides, even if the testing companies *could* build an unzappable test, it would not be a good idea. *ZAPPING* allows students to use partial knowledge to eliminate choices. Therefore, a zappable test may be even better than one that can't be *ZAPPED*. To the degree that *ZAPPING* can help students on all multiple-choice tests, the *ZAP*-ability of the ACT probably contributes to making it a reasonable predictor of success in college.

No matter how poorly you guess, any difference will always be in the positive direction. You can't hurt your score by guessing.

When you're guessing, do so quickly. A fast guess is just as good as a slow guess.

© 2005 ZAPS Learning Company. DO NOT DUPLICATE.

General Tips for the ACT

TIP 1 There is only one correct answer to each item.

The ACT editors try to make sure that every item has one and only one correct answer. Even if two answers seem OK, there is probably a technical reason why one of those answers is wrong. You might run into this problem with the Reading Test and with the style questions on the English Test. These are the two places where there will be questions that seem to have two correct answers.

Do not waste time thinking about how a second answer could be defended. The ACT editors do not intentionally create two correct answers, and the odds of a student winning an argument with ACT are quite remote. Besides, most people who can argue convincingly in favor of a wrong answer usually know which answer was considered correct in the first place. That is the answer you need to choose to get your best score. Don't waste energy making mental protests while you're taking the test.

TIP 2 Trick questions don't show up on the ACT (not on purpose, anyway).

The editorial staff at ACT tries to spot trick questions before they make it to a final form of the test. Trick questions that get by the editors are nearly always thrown out after a field test. So don't think the test is trying to trick you—not on purpose anyway.

The main point of the ACT is to separate "good" students from "poor" students. Trick questions don't help achieve this goal. Therefore, the ACT people do not intentionally include trick questions on the test. Keep in mind, however, that anybody can make a mistake, including the people at ACT.

TIP 3 There is no identifiable pattern of correct answers.

The ACT editors are very careful about making sure that the correct answers to their questions do not form a predictable pattern on the answer sheet. Even if there were a predictable pattern, only students achieving a perfect score would be able to discern it accurately. Even if you answered as few as one fourth of the questions wrong, a perfect pattern would look totally random.

Some students look for patterns whenever they run into a guessing situation. "Let's see now," they reason, "I haven't picked a D for about eight or nine questions, so I'll guess D on this one." Sound familiar? Don't waste your time trying to track patterns because there simply aren't any.

TIP 4 All choices are equally likely to occur.

On the tests that your teachers write, choice **B** or **C** will probably be correct more often than choices **A** or **D**. On the ACT, this idea does not hold true. The ACT editors pay careful attention to the frequency of answers, and they change the order of choices whenever necessary. When you're guessing, the main thing is to move quickly. A fast guess is just as good as a slow guess.

TIP 5 For you as an individual, the difficulty of the items is generally random.

You should always answer the easy questions first and skip over the harder ones. That way, if you need to guess on some items as time is running out, you'll be guessing on the items that are the hardest for you. Otherwise, you might end up losing an easy point simply because you didn't attempt all the easy items.

TIP 6 If you take control of the ACT competition, you are likely to improve your performance.

The note on page 3 points out certain elements of the test that are controlled by ACT and other elements that are under your personal control. You need to control everything you can. Your participation in this program indicates that you have taken a big step in the right direction.

TIP 7 Write freely in your test book and transfer answers carefully.

As you take the test, use *ZAPPING* strategies to draw lines through obvious wrong answers. Then transfer chosen answers immediately to the answer sheet. Be extremely careful to code the matching item number.

The Test Day

You need to know in advance the location of your test center. Find out where it is before the day of the test. If the location is not familiar, drive over a day or two before the test. Pay attention to parking options and total travel time. Colleges almost never accept applicants who get hopelessly lost and drive around in circles when they should be taking the ACT. Once you know where the test center is, make sure you get there on time. Test day is not the time to sleep in or linger over breakfast. Your photo ID is critical. If you do not have a photo ID, you will NOT be admitted unless you happen to know the person checking IDs.

On the day of the test, you should bring the following items to the testing site:

1. your admissions ticket

2. driver's license or picture I.D.

3. four sharpened No. 2 lead pencils with erasers

4. a wristwatch

5. calculator

The ACT experience drags on for more than four hours, so make certain you are comfortable when you take it. This is a performance test. You are competing with yourself more than with other students in your class. Just as in sports or arts competitions, your attention and effort on the day of the test may determine whether you attain your personal best. Your score will reflect how you do on one day and one day only.

Your performance on the ACT is important to your future, and you have a right to take it under the best possible conditions. If you are left handed, for example, insist on a left-handed desk. If the sun is in your eyes, close the curtains. If you are distracted by something in the room, do not be afraid to tell the proctors. For example, the person behind you might be coughing or sneezing, or the air conditioner might be blowing in your ear. Most proctors are really very nice people who would be glad to help you if you let them know that you have a problem with the test-taking conditions.

The English Test Competition

Description of the Test

You will read five passages that are generally devoid of any interesting content. These passages are full of errors in punctuation, grammar, usage, and sentence structure. Most of the items consist of underlined words, phrases, or sentences. You have to pick, from four choices, the correct way to write the underlined part. There are also items that are supposed to measure rhetorical skills, such as strategy, organization, and style. These items contain an underlined phrase or a box with an item number.

In addition to your total English score, your score report will provide two subscores related to the English test:

• usage/mechanics

• rhetorical skills

In terms of test-preparation, you can pretty much ignore these subscores. In fact, it's almost impossible to get any meaningful use out of them.

Instead of subscores, pay attention to which items require an understanding of the passage content and which items are dependent only on rules of proper mechanics.

Be prepared to *ZAP* almost every item.

On the ACT, in order to make sure that wrong answers are absolutely wrong, the item writer often is forced to write foils that contain fairly obvious errors. If you are watching for these, this feature of the test gives you a great advantage.

The ACT English Usage Test is constructed in such a way that quite frequently it appears that a more difficult question is being asked than is really the case. There are often additional errors introduced in the foils. The additional errors are many times easier to spot than the original difficult answer.

Competitive Scoring on the English Test

What does it take to achieve your personal best on the ACT English competition?

The following tables are based on a few assumptions:

1) You will correctly answer the questions that you know for sure. (The tables make no allowance for answer sheet marking errors.)

2) You will blind guess or *ZAP* the unknown questions. (You should leave no blanks.)

3) The raw scores on the tables (number of questions answered correctly) reflect the average results of guessing. For example, if you blind guessed on 12 questions with a 1 out of 4 chance, your expected gain would be 3 points. In actual practice you might pick up more or fewer points.

For purposes of illustration, let's assume that a student named Pat knows 25 questions for sure, and blind guesses on the other 50 questions. The average pickup from guessing would be 12.5, so Pat's Raw Score would be 38 (25 + 12.5 = 37.5). This converts to an ACT score of 15. (See the conversion table on page 84.)

With *ZAPPING*, however, Pat could raise the Raw Score an additional 4 to 12 points, converting to an ACT score as high as 19. The illustration demonstrates that with Pat's particular level of English skills, the ACT score could range anywhere from 15 to 19, depending on the application of *ZAPPING* techniques.

The "know for sure" box is an indication of your confident skill level. Use the score conversion table on page 84 to fill in the ACT scores. Notice that *ZAPPING* increases your score no matter where you start on the "know-for-sure" index.

Any particular ability level could yield a range of ACT scores. Your goal is to hit the top of your personal range. Be realistic, but don't settle for 24 if you could hit 27. And don't settle for 27 if you could hit 29.

ACT English Test

KNOW 20 for sure	55 UNKNOWNS		
Strategy	**If Blind Guess All**	**If ZAP 1 Foil All**	**If ZAP 2 Foils All**
Guess Yield	14	18	28
Raw Score	34	38	48
ACT Score*			

KNOW 25 for sure	50 UNKNOWNS		
Strategy	**If Blind Guess All**	**If ZAP 1 Foil All**	**If ZAP 2 Foils All**
Guess Yield	13	17	25
Raw Score	38	42	50
ACT Score*	15		19

KNOW 30 for sure	45 UNKNOWNS		
Strategy	**If Blind Guess All**	**If ZAP 1 Foil All**	**If ZAP 2 Foils All**
Guess Yield	11	15	23
Raw Score	41	45	53
ACT Score*			

KNOW 35 for sure	40 UNKNOWNS		
Strategy	**If Blind Guess All**	**If ZAP 1 Foil All**	**If ZAP 2 Foils All**
Guess Yield	10	13	20
Raw Score	45	48	55
ACT Score*			

KNOW 40 for sure	35 UNKNOWNS		
Strategy	**If Blind Guess All**	**If ZAP 1 Foil All**	**If ZAP 2 Foils All**
Guess Yield	9	12	18
Raw Score	49	52	58
ACT Score*			

KNOW 45 for sure	30 UNKNOWNS		
Strategy	**If Blind Guess All**	**If ZAP 1 Foil All**	**If ZAP 2 Foils All**
Guess Yield	8	10	15
Raw Score	53	55	60
ACT Score*			

KNOW 50 for sure	25 UNKNOWNS		
Strategy	**If Blind Guess All**	**If ZAP 1 Foil All**	**If ZAP 2 Foils All**
Guess Yield	6	8	13
Raw Score	56	58	63
ACT Score*			

KNOW 55 for sure	20 UNKNOWNS		
Strategy	**If Blind Guess All**	**If ZAP 1 Foil All**	**If ZAP 2 Foils All**
Guess Yield	5	7	10
Raw Score	60	62	65
ACT Score*			

KNOW 60 for sure	15 UNKNOWNS		
Strategy	**If Blind Guess All**	**If ZAP 1 Foil All**	**If ZAP 2 Foils All**
Guess Yield	4	5	8
Raw Score	64	65	68
ACT Score*			

KNOW 65 for sure	10 UNKNOWNS		
Strategy	**If Blind Guess All**	**If ZAP 1 Foil All**	**If ZAP 2 Foils All**
Guess Yield	3	3	5
Raw Score	68	68	70
ACT Score*			

*The conversion of Raw Score to ACT Score will vary slightly depending on which form of the test you happen to take. The conversion is a statistical adjustment that makes up for the unavoidable differences in the difficulty of the reading passages and test questions.

Using the Program on Your Own

Use the following tips to work on your own and prepare for the ACT English Test Competition.

1. **Do a reality check.**
   Complete one English Training Workout and determine your score using the appropriate answer key in Appendix C. As you take the test, put a star next to each item that you know for sure.

   ┌─────────────────────────────────┐
   │ **Starting Score** _____ │
   └─────────────────────────────────┘

2. **Refresh your memory.**
   Study pages 17–28 in this Study Guide.

3. **Continuing working on only one Training Workout at a time.**
   Don't try to work all of the Training Workouts in one sitting. You will get sick of it and never want to look at the ACT again. It is better to do a little bit every day over a long period than to do a couple of marathon sessions.

4. **Don't worry about your score or about timing yourself.**
   First build your skills, then work on your speed. Use the Training Workout as a diagnostic tool—to find out what types of questions you are missing most and where you need to brush up. Your score will take care of itself.

5. **Study your mistakes.**
   Look up each item you missed in the answer reviews in Appendix C. Make sure you understand why the correct answer is correct and why the wrong choices are wrong. If you are still unclear about an item after reading the answer reviews, mark that item and discuss it with one of your English teachers.

6. **Analyze your errors.**
   Are you missing mostly grammar and punctuation items (commas, semicolons, subject-verb agreement, etc.)? Or are you missing mostly style questions—like the box questions? As you are going over your answers, keep a tally of the types of questions you are missing most, then use that information to design your own study plan.

   If you're rusty on grammar and punctuation, begin by reading the answer reviews for the questions you missed. Then read through the brief grammar review on pages 22 through 28. If you are still foggy on a few of the concepts, ask a teacher to go over them with you.

   If style questions are your problem, the answer reviews will be a big help. Study the wrong choices, even on the questions you got correct. What makes the wrong choices attractive? Try to get inside the test writer's mind and see how these items are being written. Also, discuss some of the style questions with a teacher or friend. In general, the best way to improve on style questions is just to practice, practice, practice. Which brings us to the next study tip . . .

7. **Practice.**
   Complete the entire English Test in the ACT registration packet available *free* in your guidance office.

   ┌─────────────────────────────────┐
   │ **Updated Score** _____ │
   └─────────────────────────────────┘

8. **Keep practicing.**
   After analyzing your errors and doing a little reviewing, work another Training Workout. Are you still missing the same types of items? You will probably find that you have already begun to improve.

Strategies for Attacking the English Test

Specific tips for attacking the English Test are given below. As you encounter examples of each tip in your practice, write the test item numbers in the boxes provided.

TIP 1 **Watch and look out for redundancy. If it can be said with one single word, two words should not be used and applied.**

Redundancy is a big deal on the ACT, partly because it is a common problem in the writing of high school and college students. The ACT will often present two words where one will suffice. In the statement of the tip above, there are three examples of redundancy. Circle them.

The English Test likes to underline phrases such as "After they had built and constructed the doghouse . . ." or "It was her first initial appearance . . ." ACT will not make you choose between the two redundant words. They will simply give you a choice that contains only one of the words.

Examples of redundancy

A1, B29, B26

TIP 2 **Watch out for sentence fragments.**

The ACT will *never* present a sentence fragment as the correct answer choice. (If you don't know the difference between a complete sentence and a fragment, learn it. You need to know.) You'll need to check for fragments in two situations:

1. whenever you see a **period** in the underlined part, or

2. a **period** in the choices.

These are two places that a test editor would be likely to place a fragment. Whenever you see a period underlined, check both the preceding and the following sentences to make sure they are both complete. If you can't use a period, you can't substitute a semicolon.

Fragments are Homer Simpson choices. Every time you discover a fragment, you can immediately ZAP "No Change." The second part of this tip is to always check your answer to make sure your choice does not create a new fragment.

Examples of fragments

A5, A18, B27, B4

TIP 3 When you can't decide between two or three choices, choose the shorter option.

Use this tip only when guessing

ACT includes many items that ask, "What is the best way to say what is meant?" Their challenge in designing these items is to include attractive wrong choices that don't all stand out like Homer Simpson or Shaquille O'Neal. ACT often makes the wrong choices wrong by making them awkward and wordy.

What this means is that whenever you can't decide between two choices, you can *ZAP* the longer choice and pick the shorter choice. This tip DOES NOT mean that the shortest choice is *always* the right answer. Apply this idea only after *ZAPPING* for other reasons. When you get to the point where you need to guess, pick the shortest choice remaining.

Examples of shorter-is-better

A10, A11, A34, B4

TIP 4 Pay careful attention to the context in which an item appears. You can't always read just the underlined parts.

Everything that is NOT underlined on the ACT English Test is assumed to be correct. In many instances, an incorrect response is incorrect because it does not work in the context in which it appears. For this reason, it is important to carefully read the sentence or phrase preceding and following an item.

Examples of critical context

A16   A17   A18   A24   A34

TIP 5 — When two parts of one sentence are underlined, solve these two questions together.

Sometimes an item depends on the one following it, especially if two parts of the same sentence are underlined. These "double-puzzle" questions can cause a lot of frustration—and they often lead to careless errors. When you encounter a double puzzle, solve the second part first and then come back to the first part. After you get both answers, read the whole sentence again to make sure both of your choices work together.

Examples of double-puzzle questions

A2, A3   A14, A15   A17, A18

A19, A20

TIP 6 — On many items, you can *ZAP* out choices "by ear."

Take the following sentence, for example: *He seen the handwriting on the wall.* You probably know that "He seen" is inappropriate for the ACT, even if you don't know the grammatical rule. If something *sounds* wrong, it probably *is* wrong.

On the ACT, if you don't immediately know an answer, verbalize the choices to yourself. If it sounds awkward, the choice is probably wrong—*ZAP* it. The ability to "sound out" the right answer can be improved with practice. The sample tests should give you an indication of how good an ear you have for this technique.

Examples of *ZAPPING* by ear

Reread things

TIP 7
Study and compare the choices to avoid creating a new error as you correct the original error.

Often, a "good-looking" choice will introduce a change in punctuation or usage that makes the choice incorrect. This will be a problem if you don't double-check each question. After you think you see the correct answer, check the other choices to see if another answer is similar. If so, look for the difference between the two choices and reconsider which one is correct.

Examples of _ZAPPING_ to avoid creating new errors

B26
B30 (B, C, D)

TIP 8
For all underlined items, re-read the sentence after you plug in your choices.

This is a safety step to avoid making stupid mistakes. It must be done quickly or it can cause problems with your timing. The best thing to help increase your speed at this is to practice prior to the real test.

TIP 9
When the question number is in a little box, attack it in two steps.

The answers to these box questions often seem arbitrary and vague. You might find two or three choices that look sensible, or you might go through and _ZAP all four_ choices as stupid.

Attack Step 1: **Determine where in the passage you'll find the answer.**

The box questions are based either on a nearby sentence or paragraph, or on the entire passage. Read the question carefully to decide which type it is.

Examples of box questions based on a nearby sentence or paragraph

A8, A25, A31, B8, B16, B25 + B28

Examples of box questions based on the entire passage

A27   A37   B38
A28   B18

Attack Step 2: **Reread or move on, depending on the type of box question:**

- sentence or paragraph: reread, *ZAP*, move on;
- entire passage: *ZAP* and move on, DO NOT reread.

If you attack box questions according to this strategy, you should be able to immediately *ZAP* one or two choices. This will greatly reduce the amount of time you need to spend seriously considering the remaining choices.

When the number is in a little box, first determine where to find the answer, then *ZAP* and move on. Do not waste too much time on these questions.

You cannot afford to waste too much time on any one question. If a question you don't understand refers to the whole passage and you don't immediately know the answer, *ZAP* and take a guess. DO NOT go back and read the whole passage. Don't take a lot of time on any one question until after you've gone all the way through the test and answered all of the straightforward questions.

Important Note Regarding the English Test Competition

It is impossible to give one strategy that works best for all students taking the English Test. Those who know the rules of what is called "standard English" (the kind of English that is used in textbooks) may very well be able to examine the underlined part, decide how they would correct it, and look for the change among the choices given on the right.

Others may do better by reading the underlined passage and studying the choices before deciding. This gives them a hint about what kind of question is being asked and allows them to try out the different choices in the passage to see which ones either look correct or can be *ZAPPED*.

For most students, a combination of these two strategies works best. This is why practice will raise your score on the ACT English Test. By becoming more familiar with the kinds of questions that are asked, you will get a feel for which methods will get *you* a correct answer in the shortest time. Practice will show you the sort of mistakes you are likely to make and some common things to look for when trying to quickly locate errors in the underlined portions.

Grammar Review

Periods

A period ends a complete sentence. A complete sentence contains both a *subject* (who or what is doing the action) and a *predicate* (the action). If one of these is missing, you have a *sentence fragment*.

You may encounter fragments in your everyday reading, but on the ACT English Test, fragments are not acceptable.

Wrong: The moldy sandwich, a fuzzy-green and smelly entity.

> There is no predicate. What is the moldy sandwich *doing*?

Wrong: Lives in the fridge and continues to grow.

> There is no subject. We don't know *what* "lives and continues to grow."

Right: The moldy sandwich, a fuzzy-green and smelly entity, lives in the fridge and continues to grow.

> The sentence has both subject and predicate. We know what's doing the action ("the moldy sandwich"), and we know what the action is ("lives . . . and continues to grow").

Commas

A comma is simply a signal to the reader to pause. There are many rules for the use of commas, but most situations are covered by the "Fab Four" comma rules below.

1. **Commas after items in a series** – If you list three or more items in a row, you need a comma after each item in the series except the last one.

   John, Paul, George, and Ringo first recorded together in 1962.

2. **Commas after an introductory phrase** – An introductory phrase is a short phrase at the beginning of a sentence that introduces the main idea of the sentence. An introductory phrase is followed by a comma.

   By the end of 1964, the Beatles had several number one records in England.

   Though it may not have seemed overly important at the time, the "British Invasion" marked the beginning of a new era in rock-n-roll history.

3. **Commas to set off stuff that's not essential to the meaning of the sentence.**

   Parenthetical expressions – A parenthetical expression is a phrase that modifies the entire sentence. Common parenthetical expressions: "as a matter of fact," "believe me," "I am sure," "to tell the truth," and "it seems to me." Parenthetical expressions need to be set off by commas.

   The Beatles' most experimental album, in my opinion, is <u>Sgt. Pepper's Lonely Hearts Club Band</u>.

A parenthetical expression is not necessary to the meaning of the sentence; it's almost like an aside. As a matter of fact, you could remove it all together and the sentence would still be acceptable.

Right: The Beatles' most experimental album is <u>Sgt. Pepper's Lonely Hearts Club Band</u>.

Appositives – An appositive is a group of words that describes a noun or a pronoun. Appositives can appear at the beginning, middle, or end of a sentence. An appositive is set off by commas.

Paul McCartney, perhaps the most musically proficient of the Fab Four, played bass guitar.

An appositive is also not essential to the meaning of the sentence. What would happen if we just took it out?

Paul McCartney played bass guitar.

The sentence would still be acceptable.

Examples of comma misuse:

Wrong: The Beatle, who played the drums, was the last to join the group.

The words "who played the drums" are necessary for the reader to know which Beatle is being discussed; DO NOT set off with commas.

Wrong: The album, recorded just before the band's breakup, was <u>Abbey Road</u>.

The words "recorded just before the band's breakup" is necessary for the reader to know which album is being talked about; DO NOT set off with commas.

4. **Commas to separate independent clauses** – An independent clause is a string of words that can stand alone as a sentence; it contains both a subject and a predicate. When two independent clauses are joined by a comma and a *conjunction* (and, but, or, nor, for), you have a *compound sentence*.

Wrong: John, Paul, and George all played guitar, Ringo played the drums.

This sentence needs a conjunction.

Wrong: John, Paul, and George all played guitar but Ringo played the drums.

This sentence needs a comma.

Right: John, Paul, and George all played guitar, but Ringo played the drums.

This sentence has both a comma and a conjunction.

Semicolons

Semicolons are also used to link independent clauses, only *without* the use of a conjunction. A semicolon acts much like a period; everything on both sides of the semicolon must be able to stand alone as a sentence. A semicolon links two ideas more closely than a period does.

Right: Shaquille is a powerful player; his size and strength make him a formidable obstacle on the court.

Everything on both sides of the semicolon can stand alone as a sentence.

Wrong: Shaquille is a powerful player; and his size and strength make him a formidable obstacle on the court.

No conjunction is needed.

A semicolon also separates items in a list, much like a comma does. Use semicolons to make a list less confusing when there are already commas separating things within the list.

Please find the following items for the party: a stereo with both a cassette and a CD player; a birthday cake, but not the kind with icky-sweet icing; a location that has a kitchen, folding tables and chairs, and air conditioning; and plenty of invitations.

A semicolon in never interchangeable with a colon or a dash.

Colons

A colon causes a break in a sentence and calls the reader's attention to what follows. Use a colon in the following ways:

1. To explain or add emphasis to the first clause in a sentence:

   David Letterman did something no other late-night talk-show host had done: he hired his own mom as a correspondent.

2. To introduce a list following an independent clause:

   I have three simple wishes for my birthday: a year's supply of CDs, a summer vacation in Europe, and a guest appearance on <u>Friends</u>.

3. To introduce a quotation that relates strongly to the clause before it:

   In the midst of her most pressing problems, she comforted herself with a saying she'd heard since childhood: "This is a job for Kool-Aid!"

Dashes

Dashes are used to set off information that is not necessary to the meaning of the sentence, somewhat like commas do.

> The Woodstock II concert—a pale imitation of the original—was an overpriced fiasco.

> Today I went to Britches-R-Us—the one in the mall next to the music store—to shop for a new pair of jeans and a belt.

Dashes are also used to emphasize sentence elements, somewhat like colons do.

> A new scientific study has indicated a characteristic consistent in highly successful people—a love for chocolate.

Apostrophes

An apostrophe indicates possession. The apostrophe comes before the *s* when the noun is singular and after the *s* when the noun is plural.

> Dave's mom
> the girls' books
> Spike's camera
> the doctors' opinions

The possessive can also be stated as follows:

> the mother of Dave

but never:

> the mother of Dave's

When a plural noun does not already end in *s*, add an apostrophe + *s*.

> the children's toys
> the mice's cheese

With indefinite pronouns, the apostrophe always comes before the *s*.

> Everyone's expectation was that Michael would eventually return to basketball. When that might happen was anyone's guess.

Parentheses

Parentheses are used to set off information that is not essential to the meaning of the sentence.

> Who would have thought that Superman (he calls himself the "man of steel") would wear tights made by his mom?

What's the difference between commas, dashes, and parentheses?

Not much. When you want to set off information that is not essential to the meaning of the sentence, whether you use commas, dashes, or parentheses is often an editorial choice. ACT will not ask you to make such arbitrary decisions.

They WILL, however, ask you to be consistent, at least within the same sentence. The sentences below are all acceptable.

Right: Students often differ from their parents and teachers, and among themselves, on many issues.

Right: Students often differ from their parents and teachers—and among themselves—on many issues.

Right: Students often differ from their parents and teachers (and among themselves) on many issues.

Punctuation is inconsistent in the following sentences, making them unacceptable.

Wrong: Students often differ from their parents and teachers— and among themselves, on many issues.

Wrong: Students often differ from their parents and teachers, and among themselves—on many issues.

Don't mismatch them!

Common Usage Mistakes

What's wrong with this sentence?

> Everyone here should have their books.

It sounds okay to most people, but in formal speech and in writing it is more acceptable to say:

> Everyone here should have <u>his</u> book.

Since many people prefer to avoid the generic pronoun he when talking about a male or female, his or her is commonly used:

> Everyone here should have <u>his or her</u> book.

Of course, if you know the gender of the person, you would say so:

> **Somebody on the girls' basketball team forgot <u>her</u> gym bag.**

Watch for pronouns on the ACT English Test. Whenever a pronoun is underlined, quickly check for its antecedent (what it is referring to).

> **The possibilities for interacting with art, rather than gazing mutely at <u>them</u>, are endless.**

In the sentence above, *them* refers to *art* and should be changed to *it*. Other cases of pronoun-antecedent agreement are more subtle:

> **The team pays <u>their</u> own travel expenses.**

Team is a collective noun, requiring a singular verb (*pays*) and a singular pronoun. Hence, *their* would change to *its*.

The following pronouns require singular verbs and antecedents:

> **anybody, anyone, each, either, everybody, everyone, everything, neither, nobody, no one, one, somebody, someone, something**

The following pronouns always take a plural verb and antecedent:

> **both, many, several**

These pronouns can be plural or singular, depending on how they are used:

> **all, any, none, some**

For example:

> **All of you are fine students.** Plural— "All of you"

> **All of my soup is ruined.** Singular— "All of the soup"

It is easy to become confused when choosing between singular and plural forms. That's why you're likely to see a few agreement questions on the English Test. Here are two other ways that ACT makes it hard to know whether to use a singular or plural verb:

1. Fake compound subject:

> **The list of repairs and hours of labor <u>is/are</u> too large.**

This sentence sounds like the list of repairs and the hours of labor are both too large.

The only thing that is too large is the list, which happens to contain repairs and hours of labor. You wouldn't say that the hours of labor are too large, so you could tell that *list* is the subject. The correct verb would be *is*.

2. Reversed order of subject and verb. What is the subject in this sentence?

In the middle of the park stand/stands two fine statues.

Statues is the subject, so the verb should be *stand*:

Two fine statues stand in the park.

Be careful when the normal order of the sentence is reversed.

Verb Check for the ACT English Test

Regular Verbs

A regular verb is one that forms its past and past participle by adding "-ed" or "-d" to the infinitive form.

Infinitive	Past	Past Participle
kick	kicked	(have) kicked

Irregular Verbs

An irregular verb is one that forms its past and past participle in some way other than a regular verb. Some irregular verbs form the past and past participle forms by changing the vowels, some by changing the consonants, and others by making no change at all. The following is a list of common irregular verbs.

Infinitive	Past	Past Participle	Infinitive	Past	Past Participle
begin	began	(have) begun	go	went	(have) gone
blow	blew	(have) blown	ride	rode	(have) ridden
break	broke	(have) broken	ring	rang	(have) rung
bring	brought	(have) brought	run	ran	(have) run
burst	burst	(have) burst	see	saw	(have) seen
choose	chose	(have) chosen	shrink	shrank	(have) shrunk
come	came	(have) come	speak	spoke	(have) spoken
do	did	(have) done	steal	stole	(have) stolen
drink	drank	(have) drunk	swim	swam	(have) swum
drive	drove	(have) driven	take	took	(have) taken
fall	fell	(have) fallen	throw	threw	(have) thrown
freeze	froze	(have) frozen	write	wrote	(have) written
give	gave	(have) given			

The Written Essay Competition

An Essay Test is an optional section of the ACT.
It will be required by some institutions and not by others. Even if you haven't made up your mind where to apply for college, you might want to take the essay just in case you later decide to attend somewhere where it is required. The essay test will provide a score to supplement the multiple-choice questions on the English Test.

The ACT writing test allows 30 minutes to study a "prompt" and complete a short written essay. In order to help you focus on a topic, the essay test presents a situation with two points of view related to a simple question. For example, the prompt might say: "In your school district, there is a debate about what to do with money generated by the concession stands at high school athletic events. Some people want to spend the money only on athletics, while other people feel the money should be available for any extracurricular activity. In your opinion, how should the money be spent?"

Although the prompt will be different on every test, the directions following the prompt will be always be the same: "In your essay, take a position on this question. You may write about either one of the two points of view given, or you may present a different point of view on this question. Use specific reasons and examples to support your position."

The ACT prompts are confined to issues "relevant to high school students." When ACT uses that expression, what they mean is "relatively superficial." The numerous topics in your life that would be truly relevant are all off limits. The ACT prompts can't be politically loaded. So don't expect any controversial topics such as abortion or gay rights or the justification of war as a negotiating tool. You will never have to write about anything that requires deep thinking or reflection. (There's no time for that.) In order to avoid controversy, the ACT prompt will always present a debate about a politically safe issue.

The directions allow you a three-way choice:

1) support Side A

2) support Side B

3) develop a response based on your own perspective

Forget about Choice 3 above. Since the situations are always politically safe, it will be easiest to draft an essay supporting either Side A or Side B. There is no "correct," or even preferred, side. ACT will not award points more easily for one opinion over the other.

To sum up, the ACT will give you a prompt presenting two sides of an issue. You will be asked to choose a side and write an essay supporting your choice.

What is ACT looking for?

The essay test is looking for evidence of your ability to:

- take and articulate a perspective on an issue
- maintain a clear focus on the perspective throughout the essay
- explain a position by using supportive evidence and logical reasoning
- organize ideas logically
- communicate clearly in writing

Scoring the Essay

Your written answer will be scored 1–6 by at least two trained readers, for a combined score of 2–12. If the two readers disagree by 2 points or more, a third person will read your paper and make a final decision. (This scoring rule is evidence that cost-cutting and profit is more important to ACT than accurately scoring your essay. In fairness to students, a third person should score every paper where the first two readers don't agree. In order to maximize the profit margin, however, ACT refuses to do that. Before paying a third person to read your essay, the score disagreement needs to be at least 33% of the 6-point scale. This lack of reliability is tolerated only because it would be expensive to address the problem.)

The readers will score your paper using a scoring guide known as a "holistic rubric." They will award a score according to the overall quality of the essay, as well as certain aspects of writing such as the development of ideas, supporting examples, organization, word choice, and sentence structure. They are not supposed to grade based on your handwriting, but people are people. If your handwriting is extremely difficult to read, there's a good chance that one or both of the scorers will give you a lower score than your essay deserves.

Score of 6: "clear and consistent" writing competence, even if your paper includes occasional errors.

Score of 5: "reasonably consistent" writing competence, though occasional errors and lapses in quality. Your paper effectively addresses the writing assignment and is well organized and developed, including supporting ideas.

Score of 4: "adequate" writing competence with occasional errors and lapses in quality. Your paper addresses the writing task and is organized with supporting detail, but inconsistent with the correct use of language.

Score of 3: "developing" writing competence with certain weaknesses in organization, development, or supporting details. Your paper presents a steady supply of errors in grammar and sentence structure.

Score of 2: more incompetence than competence. Your paper is flawed by serious weaknesses such as poor organization, little or inappropriate detail, and frequent errors in grammar, diction, and sentence structure.

Score of 1: Ouch! Your essay is a waste of paper, demonstrating poor organization, thin development, no supporting detail, and poor use of grammar.

The ZAPS®
Six-Step Process for Attacking
the ACT Written Essay
READY–SET–GO

READY (about 5–6 minutes)

1) Study the prompt (setting and controversy)
   Carefully consider the setting and define the controversy. You need to consider:

   a) what is the issue?
   b) what are the two sides of the issue?

2) Choosing Sides—Prewriting Activity (4–5 minutes)
   Do not jump to conclusions about which side to support. Your goal is to earn a combined
   score of 12 points. You need to take whichever side will give you the best chance at this
   perfect score. The topic doesn't matter and the side you choose to support doesn't matter.
   Complete the following process BEFORE you decide which side to support.

First, imagine that you are hired to lobby for Side A. Make a quick list of anything that seems
helpful for supporting Side A. (The idea of this brainstorming activity isn't to organize your
ideas, it's to get the ideas flowing.)

Second, jump over to Side B. Again, make a quick list of anything that you could use to argue
for the position of Side B.

As soon as you have a brief list of points in support of each side, try to think of an example to
illustrate each point. The goal here is to come up with at least three strong examples on one
side or the other.

After 4–5 minutes, make a decision about which side offers you the most content for your
essay. By this point, you should already have a general idea of what you're going to write.
Remember, ACT never prefers one side over the other. The important thing is that you can
present three or four points supported by clear examples.

SET (about 5–6 minutes)

3) Organize your thoughts
In the "Ready" stage, you chose one side to support. You also listed a few positive reasons for your choice, and you identified some supporting examples.

Begin to organize your thoughts into a logical sequence. The ideal ACT essay may be constructed in five paragraphs:

Paragraph 1) Introduction and thesis statement (a clear statement of your position)

Paragraph 2) Topic sentence for strongest supporting reason and example to illustrate

Paragraph 3) Topic sentence for second supporting reason and example to illustrate

Paragraph 4) Topic sentence for third supporting reason and example to illustrate

Paragraph 5) Wrap Up—Conclusion (restatement of thesis sentence)

GO (about 18–20 minutes)

4. Write the first draft
Use your outline to write a first draft. Do not be concerned at this point about precise grammar or sentence structure. Start writing and keep writing. Be specific rather than vague. Support each of your main points with one or two details or examples. Don't be afraid to use similes and metaphors to strengthen your writing. You do not have a lot of time, so get your first draft on paper and move to the next step.

5. Read what you wrote
Stop writing and read your first draft. Does it seem logical and literate? Would someone else understand what you have written? Did you vary the sentence structure? Does your essay flow without a struggle?

6. Edit your work
Now edit your paper for correct grammar, sentence structure, word usage, subject-verb agreement, spelling, and punctuation. Polish the rough spots with your attention on detail.

ACT Essay Traps to Avoid

Many students hurt their essay score by making fairly predictable errors. DO NOT do any of the following:

- Neglect to re-read the prompt as you are writing.
- Jump into examples without first stating your position.
- Try to argue both sides of the issue in the hopes of sounding balanced.
- Write with giant handwriting just to fill up the space.
- Express strong opinions without supporting examples or detail.
- Use examples that don't relate to your supporting points.
- Forget to write a final paragraph that sums up your position.

How to Avoid the ACT Essay Traps

The ideal ACT essay may be written in five paragraphs, as outlined in Step Three of the ZAPS Six-Step Process. The highest scores will be given to your essay if you:

- Stick precisely to the topic described in the prompt.
- Clearly state which side are you supporting.
- Formulate a clear and precise thesis statement.
- Present 3–4 reasons supporting your position.
- Give an example or supporting detail for each reason.
- Write a final sentence that neatly summarizes your position.
- Edit your essay so that it flows easily for the reader.
- Edit for correct grammar and punctuation.

ZAP-ACT™ ESSAY PRACTICE PROMPT #1

A soft drink company has offered the school district a large sum of money in exchange for exclusive control of all vending machines and the right to advertise on school property. In your opinion, should the district accept or refuse this contract?

In your essay, take a position on this question. You may write about either one of the two points of view given, or you may present a different point of view on this question. Use specific reasons and examples to support your position.

ZAP-ACT™ ESSAY PRACTICE PROMPT #2

A group of activists in your state wants to require every person below the age of 18 to acquire a high school diploma before applying for a driver's license. Many people believe that this requirement infringes on their rights. In your opinion, should a high school degree be a requirement of receiving a driver's license?

In your essay, take a position on this question. You may write about either one of the two points of view given, or you may present a different point of view on this question. Use specific reasons and examples to support your position.

ZAP-ACT™ ESSAY PRACTICE PROMPT #3

Your school board is debating whether to approve plans for a girls-only high school. Any female student would have a choice whether to attend either the regular coed school, or a separate-but-equal school for girls. In your opinion, should the plan be approved?

In your essay, take a position on this question. You may write about either one of the two points of view given, or you may present a different point of view on this question. Use specific reasons and examples to support your position.

ZAP-ACT™ ESSAY PRACTICE PROMPT #4

Parents and teachers in your community have requested that high school students should be allowed to work a maximum of 15 hours per week. Opponents feel there should be no limit. The school board is debating the issue. In your opinion, should the district place limits on how many hours a student may work?

In your essay, take a position on this question. You may write about either one of the two points of view given, or you may present a different point of view on this question. Use specific reasons and examples to support your position.

ZAP-ACT™ ESSAY PRACTICE PROMPT #5

The City Counsel is considering a plan to issue youth work permits only to teenagers who are in good standing with the local high school. Work permits would be denied to any high school drop out under the age of 18. In your opinion is the plan a good idea?

In your essay, take a position on this question. You may write about either one of the two points of view given, or you may present a different point of view on this question. Use specific reasons and examples to support your position.

ZAP-ACT™ ESSAY PRACTICE PROMPT #6

A group of parents and teachers feel that the school district should require a minimum grade point average of 2.5 for any student to participate in any high school athletic competition. In your opinion, would this be a wise policy?

In your essay, take a position on this question. You may write about either one of the two points of view given, or you may present a different point of view on this question. Use specific reasons and examples to support your position.

ZAP-ACT™ ESSAY PRACTICE PROMPT #7

A group of citizens in your community is urging the school district to stop endorsing any activity that does not allow equal participation for all students. Specifically, they believe that the high school should not sell year books or class rings because not all students can afford to purchase these items. Their opponents believe that this is a "free market" issue and that the district should not get involved. In your opinion, should schools participate in the marketing and distribution of commercial products?

In your essay, take a position on this question. You may write about either one of the two points of view given, or you may present a different point of view on this question. Use specific reasons and examples to support your position.

The Mathematics Test Competition

Description of the Test

You get to solve 60 problems in 60 minutes. Are you ready? Don't worry. These are totally ordinary problems. Most of them will be fairly easy if you've completed at least one algebra class. And you don't need to get them all right to get a high ACT score. Even if you miss half of the items, you may still score around a 20. Think about that. A score of 50% on a classroom test would usually yield an F. But on the ACT, 50% is right at the national average. So don't think of this test the way you think of a classroom test.

Five content areas are included on the ACT Math Test. These are listed on page 1 of this Study Guide. You don't need to memorize any complex formulas, and the test does not require a lot of computation.

In addition to your total math score, your score report will provide three subscores related to the ACT Math Test:

• pre-algebra/elementary algebra

• intermediate algebra/coordinate geometry

• plane geometry/trigonometry

If these categories seem arbitrary to you, it's because they are. The subscores will be of little or no value in terms of preparing for the test. Just as with English, it is highly unlikely that anyone in the universe will care about any of your scores except your total.

Why Study for the Math Test?

If one hundred students with equal math ability were to take the ACT next Saturday, they would not all get the same score. Why? Because the test is not a perfect measure of math ability. A lot of the score has to do with how good you are at taking tests. And some of the score has to do with whether you're having a good or bad day. Preparation and practice can help you achieve a better score than unprepared students who have equal or superior math ability. On the other hand, if you don't practice in advance, you could score worse than some students who aren't as good as you in real math classes.

Competitive Scoring on the Mathematics Test

What does it take to achieve your personal best on the ACT math competition?

The following tables are based on a few assumptions:

1) You will correctly answer the problems that you know for sure. (The tables make no allowance for answer sheet marking errors.)

2) You will blind guess or *ZAP* the unknown problems. (You should leave no blanks.)

3) The raw scores on the tables (number of problems answered correctly) reflect the average results of guessing. For example, if you blind guessed on 15 questions with a 1 out of 5 chance, your expected gain would be 3 points. In actual practice, you might pick up more or fewer points.

For purposes of illustration, let's assume that our friend Pat knows 35 questions for sure, and blind guesses on the other 25 questions. The average pickup from guessing would be 5, so Pat's Raw Score would be 40 (35 + 5). This converts to an ACT score of 24. (See the conversion table on page 84.)

With *ZAPPING*, however, Pat could raise the Raw Score as much as 8 more points, converting to an ACT score as high as 27. The illustration demonstrates that with Pat's particular level of math ability, the ACT score could range anywhere from 24 to 27, depending on the application of *ZAPPING* techniques.

The "know for sure" box is an indication of your confident skill level. Use the score conversion table on page 84 to fill in the ACT scores. Notice that *ZAPPING* increases your score no matter where you start on the "know-for-sure" index.

Any particular ability level could yield a range of ACT scores. Your goal is to hit the top of your personal range. Be realistic, but don't settle for 20 if you could hit 24. And don't settle for 24 if you could hit 28.

ACT Mathematics Test

KNOW 10 for sure	50 UNKNOWNS			
Strategy	If Blind Guess All	If ZAP 1 Foil All	If ZAP 2 Foils All	If ZAP 3 Foils All
Guess Yield	10	13	17	25
Raw Score	20	23	27	35
ACT Score*				

KNOW 15 for sure	45 UNKNOWNS			
Strategy	If Blind Guess All	If ZAP 1 Foil All	If ZAP 2 Foils All	If ZAP 3 Foils All
Guess Yield	9	11	15	23
Raw Score	24	26	30	38
ACT Score*				

KNOW 20 for sure	40 UNKNOWNS			
Strategy	If Blind Guess All	If ZAP 1 Foil All	If ZAP 2 Foils All	If ZAP 3 Foils All
Guess Yield	8	10	13	20
Raw Score	28	30	33	40
ACT Score*				

KNOW 25 for sure	35 UNKNOWNS			
Strategy	If Blind Guess All	If ZAP 1 Foil All	If ZAP 2 Foils All	If ZAP 3 Foils All
Guess Yield	7	9	12	18
Raw Score	32	34	37	43
ACT Score*				

KNOW 30 for sure	30 UNKNOWNS			
Strategy	If Blind Guess All	If ZAP 1 Foil All	If ZAP 2 Foils All	If ZAP 3 Foils All
Guess Yield	6	8	10	15
Raw Score	36	38	40	45
ACT Score*				

KNOW 35 for sure	25 UNKNOWNS			
Strategy	If Blind Guess All	If ZAP 1 Foil All	If ZAP 2 Foils All	If ZAP 3 Foils All
Guess Yield	5	6	8	13
Raw Score	40	41	43	48
ACT Score*	24			27

KNOW 40 for sure	20 UNKNOWNS			
Strategy	If Blind Guess All	If ZAP 1 Foil All	If ZAP 2 Foils All	If ZAP 3 Foils All
Guess Yield	4	5	7	10
Raw Score	44	45	47	50
ACT Score*				

KNOW 45 for sure	15 UNKNOWNS			
Strategy	If Blind Guess All	If ZAP 1 Foil All	If ZAP 2 Foils All	If ZAP 3 Foils All
Guess Yield	3	4	5	8
Raw Score	48	49	50	53
ACT Score*				

KNOW 50 for sure	10 UNKNOWNS			
Strategy	If Blind Guess All	If ZAP 1 Foil All	If ZAP 2 Foils All	If ZAP 3 Foils All
Guess Yield	2	3	3	5
Raw Score	52	53	53	55
ACT Score*				

KNOW 55 for sure	5 UNKNOWNS			
Strategy	If Blind Guess All	If ZAP 1 Foil All	If ZAP 2 Foils All	If ZAP 3 Foils All
Guess Yield	1	1	2	3
Raw Score	56	56	57	58
ACT Score*				

*The conversion of Raw Score to ACT Score will vary slightly depending on which form of the test you happen to take. The conversion is a statistical adjustment that makes up for the unavoidable differences in the difficulty of any particular set of math problems.

Using the Program on Your Own

Use the following tips to work on your own and prepare for the ACT Math Test.

1. **Do a reality check.**
   Complete one Mathematics Training Workout and determine your score using the answer key in Appendix C. As you take the test, put a star next to each problem that you know for sure.

Starting Score _____

2. **Refresh your memory.**
   Study pages 44–58 in this Study Guide.

3. **Continuing working only one Training Workout at a time.**
   Don't try to work all of the Training Workouts in one sitting.

4. **Don't worry about your score or about timing yourself.**
   First build your skills, then work on your speed. Use the Training Workout as a diagnostic tool. Your score will take care of itself.

5. **Study your mistakes.**
   Look up each item you missed in the answer reviews in Appendix C. Make sure you understand why the correct answer is correct and why the wrong choices are wrong.

   Rework the problems you missed. This will reinforce what you learned from the problem; otherwise, you will be likely to have trouble with the same type of problem the next time.

6. **Classify your errors (see pages 49 and 50).**
   Classify each error as an E1, E2, or E3. Then go one step further in analyzing your E2s. Are you missing mostly algebra? Geometry? Or are you rusty on some basic arithmetic stuff?

   As you are going over your answers, keep a tally of the types of E2 errors you are making, then use that information to design your own study plan. Here are a few tips for creating a personalized math review:

   • Read the explanations for the problems in the question reviews.

   • Rework the problems you missed or were unsure of.

   • Study the Mathematics Concepts and Trigonometry Review on pages 52 through 58 of this Study Guide.

   • Review old math textbooks, working the chapter reviews at the end of each chapter.

   • Ask a teacher to re-explain concepts that are still fuzzy to you.

   • Form a study group.

7. **Practice.**
   Complete the entire Math Test in the ACT registration packet, available *free* in your guidance office.

Updated Score _____

8. **Keep practicing.**

The more you work on ACT math problems, the better you will get. Practicing will do several things for you. *It will increase your familiarity with the test.* The same types of problems show up again and again on the ACT Math Test, only the situations are different. For instance, instead of having Bill buy records, they may have Sue buying books. The more you practice, the more prepared you will be for the types of problems you will see. *Your math skills will also improve, as well as your speed at working the actual problems.* Most importantly, *practicing will help you reduce anxiety*, which is one of the chief causes of E1 errors.

A Word About Calculators

Don't get too excited about using your calculator on the ACT math test—it will not guarantee a better score or make up for the math class you slept through last year. To get a good score, you need a solid understanding of basic math concepts. You must be able to work through the math problems, not just plug a few numbers into your calculator.

The advantage of a calculator is that it may increase your speed in working through some of the problems. However, a calculator will not make up for lack of math preparation. The best use of your calculator is to check your answers.

Begin practicing with your calculator NOW.

If you don't have a calculator, don't wait until the night before the test to go out and buy one. The calculator you take with you to the test must be one that you are thoroughly familiar with. Even the simplest calculator can have its own peculiarities. Begin practicing with your calculator NOW so that you are comfortable with it. You don't want any surprises on test day.

Don't try to use your calculator on every problem.

Many of the ACT math problems require no calculation at all, only a thorough understanding of math concepts. Other problems can be worked more quickly by simply thinking through the information given. If you rely on your calculator for every problem, you can end up wasting a lot of time. Practice to find out which types of problems can be solved more quickly with the aid of a calculator. First *think through* what needs to be done with the problem. What steps will you need to take? Is there a shorter way to find the answer?

Strategies for Attacking the Mathematics Test

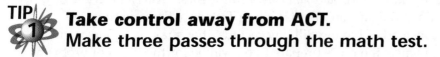

TIP 1 Take control away from ACT.
Make three passes through the math test.

FIRST PASS

- Go from item 1 through item 60, working only the problems you can do quickly and easily.

- Let nothing slow you down—skip any time-consuming problems.

- Aim for 100% correct on First Pass items.

- Be extremely careful—don't make stupid mistakes.

SECOND PASS

- Go back to the beginning and start over.

- Work the harder items that you know how to work.

- Skip or guess at the demons.

THIRD PASS

- If you have time, try to work the most difficult problems.

- Guess at the items you can't work.

- DO NOT leave any BLANKS!

Usually, time will be running out by the end of your second pass. Don't worry about this. It is *NOT* critical for you to work every problem on the math test. It *IS* critical, however, for you to check your work in order to avoid dumb mistakes.

The first step of taking control of the math test is to shorten it up to fit your personal situation. Get real with yourself; if your starting score is around 18–20, don't fantasize about moving up to a 30. Instead, think in terms of a couple of points at a time. The number of problems you need to work and double-check depends on your target score. The following table shows what you need to do to hit various target levels.

Reasonable Target ACT Math Score	To take control of the Math test, you need to be . . .
30–31	. . . correct on 54 problems, and you can blind guess on the remaining 6 problems.
28–29	. . . correct on 50 problems, and you can blind guess on the remaining 10 problems.
25–26	. . . correct on 40 problems, and you can blind guess on the remaining 20 problems.
21–22	. . . correct on 30 problems, and you can blind guess on the remaining 30 problems.
18–19	. . . correct on 20 problems, and you can blind guess on the remaining 40 problems.

For example, if your reasonable target is an ACT math score of 21, you need to use as much time as necessary to work and double check 30 of the 60 problems—even if it takes you 58 minutes. In the remaining minutes, blind guess the other 30 answers. On the average, you'll pick the right answer about 6 times out of 30 blind guesses. Your raw score will be about 36 and your ACT score will be about 21.

The key to making this system work is to be perfect on the number of problems that you work and double-check. Careless mistakes can ruin your ACT math score.

TIP 2 Study the directions in advance.

Just as with all the ACT subtests, the directions for math items are the same on every form of the ACT.

The ACT is called a "standardized test." On every standardized test, the thing that's "standard" is the administration. This includes such variables as the length of test time, the answer sheet, the testing conditions, the time of year, *and* the directions. If the directions were varied from one administration to the next, the scores would not be meaningful. In order to report valid scores, the people at ACT must be absolutely consistent in the presentation of directions. That is why you don't need to read the directions during the test—provided, of course, that you study them in advance.

TIP 3 Every problem has one and only one correct answer.

If you know how to do the math, do it. The fastest way through these problems is usually to do the math and then find your answer among the choices. Keep a clear head as you check the format of the choices. The "best" method of solution sometimes depends on how the choices are presented.

TIP 4 Do not believe any coaching that suggests you can easily find the answers by applying a series of simple tricks.

The ACT editors go to great lengths to make sure that they catch any items where tricks make a difference. As a result of their careful editing, the application of tricks is usually more difficult than the straight math.

TIP 5 Check your work on every problem.

It is far more important to avoid dumb mistakes than it is to race to the end of the test. There is no bonus for finishing early.

Most students check their work only if they don't find their answer among the choices. All of the problems on the ACT Math Test have predictable errors. What this means is that the common wrong answers will be included among the choices.

TIP 6 Write or draw freely in your book (but not on your answer sheet, of course).

You will not be allowed to use scratch paper when you take the test, so don't use scratch paper when you practice. *Get in the habit of writing all over the test book.* There are four purposes for this:

1. to make sketches and to compute or figure your answers;

2. to keep track of your answers, so you can backtrack if you mess up on your answer sheet;

3. to assist with your concentration on each item;

4. to help clarify the math problem that you need to solve.

TIP 7 Use the *PLUG-n-ZAP* method.

Take a look at the following problem:

45. The downtown area of Springville has parking places for 1,300 cars in three parking garages. Garage *A* will hold 200 more cars than Garage *B* and 150 less than Garage *C*. How many cars will Garage *A* hold?

   A. 600

   B. 450

   C. 400

   D. 250

   E. 200

If you had no idea how to set up this problem, you could start by plugging in the choices and working backwards. What this means is that you *assume* one of the answers is correct and then check to see if everything fits.

Notice that the choices are placed in order from greatest to least. When plugging in choices, start with the middle one—**C**. If you *assume* **C** is the answer, does everything fit together? If it does, then **C** is probably correct. If **C** is too big or too small, you can eliminate it, and you can also eliminate two more choices based on your findings.

If we plug in **C** for Garage A . . .

Step 1:

Garage A = **400**

Garage B = A − 200 = **400** − 200 = 200

Garage C = A + 150 = **400** + 150 = 550

Step 2:

Garage A + Garage B + Garage C = 1,300

  400   +   200   +   550   = 1,300

(this doesn't fit) 1150 ≠ 1,300

So, **C** must be too small. *ZAP* it. You can also *ZAP* **D** and **E**—they also will be too small.

  A. 600
  B. 450
  C̸. 400
  D̸. 250
  E̸. 200

Now you're down to a 50/50 chance. Try **A**. If A doesn't work, you don't have to try **B**—it would be the only choice left. With the PLUG-n-*ZAP* method, you only have to try out two choices, instead of all 5.

Examples of Plug-n-*ZAP*

TIP 8   Almost every test will have at least one or two problems involving averages.

Don't expect ACT to ask you a question like, "What is the average of 24, 16, and 35?" ACT average problems look more like this:

> If a salesperson sells four cars for an average cost of $10,000 each, and three of the cars sell for $8,400 each, what is the cost of the fourth car?

> **OR**

> A total of 60 sophomores and juniors were given a history test. The 45 juniors had an average score of 85 while the 15 sophomores had an average of 90. What was the average score for all 60 students who took the test?

You need to know how to work average problems given to you in many different forms. To solve these problems, you need to identify three variables: the Total, Average, and Number. (Just think of getting a TAN.)

Usually, the ACT will give you two of these pieces and you must use the information to determine the third piece. Sometimes, you need to add a list of numbers or do some small computation to get the first two pieces before you can go after the third piece. Depending on which piece is missing, you need to use one of the forms of the following formula:

$$\left(\frac{T}{A\,|\,N}\right)$$

1. The Total is the Average times the Number $T = A \bullet N$

2. The Average is the Total divided by the Number $A = \dfrac{T}{N}$

3. The Number is the Total divided by the Average $N = \dfrac{T}{A}$

Examples of average problems

TIP 9   The ACT figures are sometimes NOT drawn to scale.

This means that a side with length 8 may not be drawn exactly twice as long as a side with length 4. So, when you are given the length of one side, you cannot necessarily find the length of other sides simply by measuring. When drawings are distorted, it's usually because an accurate drawing would make the correct answer too obvious. If it's possible, make a more accurate drawing to see if you can figure out the answer more easily.

Types of Errors

As you prepare for the ACT, you need to pay attention to the reason behind every incorrect answer. You will probably be surprised to discover that about half of your errors are on problems you know how to solve. Under the pressure of time, it is common to make careless mistakes. After you complete each practice test, note which error type is responsible for each wrong answer.

Error 1 (E1): The dumb, careless mistake, or the misunderstood question.

This type of error is common for students at all levels of math ability. It occurs most frequently on the easiest items. E1 errors include things like carelessness, sloppiness, or mistakes on basic facts and simple computation. The number of your E1 errors should make you realize how important it is to be careful and check your work.

With certain types of ACT questions, you might have trouble figuring out exactly what you are supposed to do. This happens frequently with story problems. The solution is to practice over and over on your practice tests. After you finish a test once, don't feel you're done with it. If you work the same items three or four times, you will still be getting something out of your effort.

In addition to carelessness, E1 errors are often related to how intimidated you are by the ACT. If you begin the math test in a cold sweat, it will not be possible to think clearly and visualize every problem. The solution to this malady is practice and familiarity. By the time you have completed all of your practice tests, you should find the ACT much less intimidating. On the other hand, if you don't take the test seriously, you can also get into trouble. The idea is to be serious, but not stressed out about it.

> **For many students, E1 Errors are the most frequent type of error they make on the ACT. E1 Errors are NOT math mistakes. They are test-taking mistakes.**

Error 2 (E2): The "I can't remember" problem.

These problems are recognizable, and you understand the question, but you can't quite recall how to do the math. For example, you might remember problems in math classes such as $(x^2)(x^3) = ?$, but you can't remember whether to add or multiply the exponents. (You add them.)

The way to minimize this type of error is to review the chapter tests in a pre-algebra, geometry or algebra math book. The review will refresh your memory and minimize E2 mistakes, and it should help reduce E1 errors as well.

> **The activity of cramming for the ACT is probably worthless—in most cases. However, if you are making a lot of E2 math mistakes, a last-minute review of old math textbooks should help you reduce this type of error.**

Error 3 (E3): The "never had it" problem.

Unlike the problems that cause E2 errors, these problems require math that is completely unfamiliar to you. If your test date is scheduled in the next month or so, don't pretend that you're suddenly going to learn a whole new course in mathematics.

If you have attended a normal series of math courses, chances are good that you will see only three to five E3 situations on any one form of the ACT. If you have not been enrolled in math courses, you will need to score as many points as possible on the easier items. But don't try to cram a whole math course into one month of preparation.

Your Personal Error-Type Table

After you complete each practice math test, classify your errors as E1s, E2s, or E3s. Then count the number of each type of error and record it in the table below. Use the table to help focus your practice sessions.

	E1	E2	E3
Training Workout A			
Training Workout B			
Training Workout C			
Training Workout D			
Training Workout E			
Training Workout F			
Training Workout G			
Training Workout H			
Training Workout I			

The History of Story Problems

Research indicates that story problems were created in the early 17th century by the sadistic tutor of a well-known royal family. The tutor had earlier been reprimanded for making his students sit in ground glass while performing trigometric functions. In a creative effort to avoid further punishment, the tutor invented something called "story problems" that could be inflicted on his young pupils without eliciting the sympathy of the king and queen. This method of tormenting and confusing students enjoyed immediate and popular acceptance among frustrated math teachers who had previously relied on a paddle or hickory whip to establish the proper attitude toward mathematics. . . . *Believe it, or not.*

How to Attack Story Problems

The ACT usually presents simple math in the context of word problems. The method you use to attack these problems must remain flexible because the best approach depends on the problem. Keep a clear head. Do not let yourself get muddled up. If a problem looks like it's from another planet, skip it and try the next one. In general, keeping in mind that you'll need to be flexible, you should handle story problems in six steps:

1. **Read the "question" part of the problem first.** Underline it. This will give you a mental framework or context for the presentation of the question.

2. **Read the whole problem from the beginning** and try to see the action or operation that is taking place. Sometimes the wording is more complicated than seems reasonable, but this is because of the need for precision in the test item. The complicated wording is less of a problem if you follow the advice in Step 1.

3. **Pull the math from the problem.** Make a sketch or write notes or write a number sentence—anything to get you *into* the situation and to get the math *out* of the situation.

4. **Re-read the problem to make sure your math works.** (This procedure is one way to avoid E1 and E2 errors.)

5. **Do the math.** Make sure you don't get into complex equations or computation. If you find yourself in the middle of a long, drawn-out process, you're probably working the problem incorrectly.

6. **Check your answer by plugging it into the original problem.** Even if you can't trace the math, or if you're running out of time, you must at least check your answer to make sure it's logical in the context of the problem. Also, refer back to step one and make sure you have answered the question being asked.

Mathematics Concepts Review

Adding Even and Odd Numbers

even + even = even
odd + odd = even
even + odd = odd

Multiplying Even and Odd Numbers

even $\times$ even = even
even $\times$ odd = even
odd $\times$ odd = odd

Absolute Value

Absolute value is the numerical value of a number when the positive or negative sign is not considered. The absolute value of a number is always positive (except when the number is zero) and is written as $|x|$.

Fractions

Addition
To add fractions, change all denominators to their lowest common denominator (LCD), then add the numerators.

Example: $\frac{1}{3} + \frac{2}{5} = \frac{5}{15} + \frac{6}{15} = \frac{11}{15}$

Subtraction
To subtract fractions, change all denominators to their LCD, then subtract the numerators.

Example: $\frac{3}{4} - \frac{1}{2} = \frac{3}{4} - \frac{2}{4} = \frac{1}{4}$

Multiplication
To multiply fractions, multiply the numerators, then multiply the denominators.

Example: $\frac{3}{5} \times \frac{2}{3} = \frac{6}{15}$

Division
To divide fractions, flip the second fraction upside down and multiply.

Example: $\frac{1}{4} \div \frac{1}{3} = \frac{1}{4} \times \frac{3}{1} = \frac{3}{4}$

Percents

Percent means hundredths, or number out of 100.

Examples: $\frac{30}{100} = 30\%$

2 is 25% of 8 because $\frac{2}{8} = \frac{25}{100} = 25\%$

Converting Decimals to Percents
Move the decimal two places to the right and insert a percent sign.

Examples: $.09 = 9\%$ $.85 = 85\%$

$2.13 = 213\%$ $.007 = .7\%$

Converting a Fraction $\frac{x}{y}$ to a Percent

$$\frac{x}{y} = \frac{z}{100}$$

$$z = 100\left(\frac{x}{y}\right)$$

Example: $\frac{2}{5} = \frac{z}{100}$

$$z = 100\left(\frac{2}{5}\right)$$

$$z = 40\%$$

Finding the Percent of a Number
Change the percent to a decimal and multiply.

Example: What is 20% of 50?

$.20 \times 50 = 10.00 = 10$

Ratios

Read "m is to n" and written $m{:}n$ or m/n.

Proportions

Written as two ratios that are equal to each other. Read "c is to d as s is to t" and written as:

$$\frac{c}{d} = \frac{s}{t}$$

Exponents

Positive Exponents

$$3^4 = 3 \times 3 \times 3 \times 3 = 81$$

Negative Exponents

$$2^{-3} = \frac{1}{2^3} = \frac{1}{8}$$

NOTE: $x^1 = x$ and $x^0 = 1$ when x is any number other than 0.

Multiplication/Division

To multiply, if the base numbers are the same, keep the base number and add the exponents.

Example: $4^3 \times 4^2 = 4^5$

To divide, if the base numbers are the same, keep the base number and subtract the second exponent from the first.

Example: $5^7 \div 5^3 = 5^4$

When the base numbers are not the same, first simplify each number with an exponent and then multiply or divide.

Examples: $4^2 \times 3^3 = 16 \times 27 = 432$

$$4^2 \div 2^2 = 16 \div 4 = 4$$

Addition/Subtraction

Whether the base numbers are the same or not, you must simplify each number with an exponent before performing the operation.

Examples: $5^2 + 3^3 = 25 + 27 = 52$

$$6^2 - 2^4 = 36 - 16 = 20$$

NOTE: If a number with an exponent is raised to another power, keep the base number and multiply the exponents.

Example: $(6^3)^4 = 6^{12}$

Averages

When solving averages problems, remember the TAN:

$$\textbf{T}\text{otal} = \text{Average} \times \text{Number}$$

$$\textbf{A}\text{verage} = \frac{\text{Total}}{\text{Number}}$$

$$\textbf{N}\text{umber} = \frac{\text{Total}}{\text{Average}}$$

Algebra Concepts

Multiplying Polynomials

To multiply two binomials (an algebraic expression with two terms), use the F.O.I.L. method. F.O.I.L. stands for **F**irst, **O**utermost, **I**nnermost, and **L**ast.

F.O.I.L.

Step 1: Multiply the **F**irst terms from each expression.

Step 2: Multiply the **O**utermost terms.

Step 3: Multiply the **I**nnermost terms.

Step 4: Multiply the **L**ast terms.

Step 5: Simplify if necessary.

Example: $(2m - n)(4m + 3n)$

Step 1: **First:**

$$(2m - n)(4m + 3n) = \textbf{8}\textit{m}^2$$

Step 2: **Outermost:**

$$(2m - n)(4m + 3n) = 8m^2 + \textbf{6}\textit{mn}$$

Step 3: **Innermost:**

$$(2m - n)(4m + 3n) = 8m^2 + 6mn - \textbf{4}\textit{mn}$$

Step 4: **Last:**

$$(2m - n)(4m + 3n) = 8m^2 + 6mn - 4mn - \textbf{3}\textit{n}^2$$

Step 5: **Simplify:**

$$8m^2 + 6mn - 4mn - 3n^2 = \textbf{8}\textit{m}^2 + \textbf{2}\textit{mn} - \textbf{3}\textit{n}^2$$

Factoring Quadratic Equations

To factor a quadratic equation in the form $x^2 + Bx + C = 0$, find two numbers r and s such that: $r + s = B$ and $r \times s = C$

Example: $x^2 + 7x + 10 = 0$

What two numbers when added together would equal 7 and when multiplied together would equal 10? 2 and 5

$(x + 2)(x + 5) = 0$

Solving Quadratic Equations

To solve a quadratic equation (one that can be written as $Ax^2 + Bx + C = 0$):

Step 1: Set all terms equal to zero.

Step 2: Factor.

Step 3: Set each factor equal to zero.

Step 4: Solve each of these equations.

Example: $x^2 + 7x = -10$

Step 1: $x^2 + 7x + 10 = 0$

Step 2: $(x + 2)(x + 5) = 0$

Step 3: $x + 2 = 0$ *or* $x + 5 = 0$

Step 4: $x = -2$ *or* $x = -5$

To check your work, insert your answer in the original equation.

Inequalities

Treat inequalities (such as $7x + 4 > 32$) just like equations, with one exception: When multiplying or dividing both sides by a negative number, you must **reverse** the direction of the sign.

Quadratic Formula

$$x = \frac{-b \pm \sqrt{b^2 - 4ac}}{2a}$$

Coordinate Graphs

On the graph below, the horizontal and vertical lines are called the *coordinate axes*, or the *x-axis* and *y-axis*. The coordinate graph is divided into *quadrants*, labeled here by Roman numerals I, II, III, and IV. The numbers in parentheses (called *ordered pairs*) represent points on a plane. (0, 0) represents the *origin*.

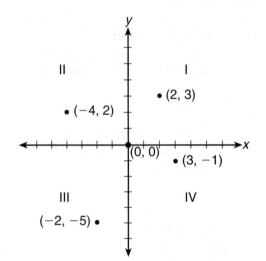

For point $(-4, 2)$, -4 is the *x-coordinate* and shows how far the point lies left or right of the origin; 2 is the *y-coordinate* and shows how far the point lies up or down.

Slope of a Line

To find the slope of a line in a coordinate plane, use the following formula:

the difference in the *y*-coordinates
of any two points on the line

──────────────────────────────

the difference in the *x*-coordinates
of any two points on the line

or simply stated: $\dfrac{\text{rise}}{\text{run}}$ or $\dfrac{y_2 - y_1}{x_2 - x_1}$

Linear Equations

Standard Form $Ax + By + C = 0$

Point-Slope Form $(y - y_1) = m(x - x_1)$

Slope-Intercept Form $y = mx + b$

Equation of a Circle

Standard form for the equation of a circle with center (h, k) and radius r:

$$(x - h)^2 + (y - k)^2 = r^2$$

Geometry Concepts

Lines and Angles

Parallel lines remain the same distance apart FOREVER. They never meet. Parallel lines are denoted by the symbol $\parallel$.

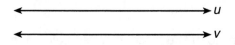

Perpendicular lines intersect to form right angles and are denoted by the symbol $\perp$.

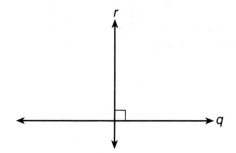

A **right angle** measures 90 degrees.

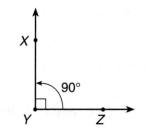

A **straight angle** measures 180 degrees.

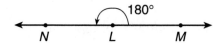

Adjacent angles share a common vertex and a common side.

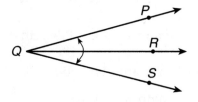

Complementary angles are two angles with measures totalling 90 degrees.

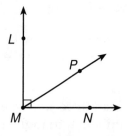

Supplementary angles are two angles with measures totalling 180 degrees.

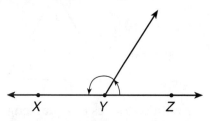

When two lines intersect, four angles are formed. The angles opposite each other are called **vertical angles** and their measures are equal. In the example below, the measures of angles 1 and 3 are equal, and the measures of angles 2 and 4 are equal.

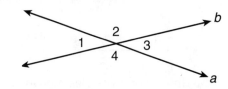

An example of **two parallel lines cut by a third line** (called a *transversal*) is shown below.

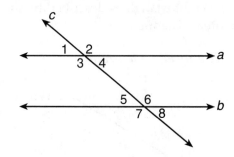

Angles 1 and 5 are called **corresponding angles** and their measures are equal.

Angles 3 and 6 are called **alternate interior angles** and their measures are equal.

Angles 2 and 7 are called **alternate exterior angles** and their measures are equal.

Triangles

The sum of the measures of the angles of a triangle is always 180 degrees.

The sum of the lengths of any two sides of a triangle must be greater than the length of the third side.

A triangle with all three sides the same length is called an **equilateral triangle**. Each angle of an equilateral triangle measures 60 degrees.

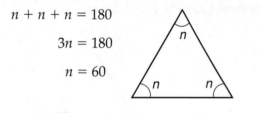

$$n + n + n = 180$$
$$3n = 180$$
$$n = 60$$

A triangle with two sides of equal length is called an **isosceles triangle**. Two of the angles in an isosceles triangle (those opposite the equal sides) are also of equal measure.

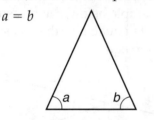

$$a = b$$

A triangle with one of its angles measuring 90 degrees is called a **right triangle**. The relationship between the lengths of the three sides of a right triangle is described by the Pythagorean Theorem.

The Pythagorean Theorem

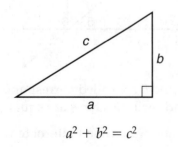

$$a^2 + b^2 = c^2$$

Example: If $a = 6$, $b = 8$, and $c = 10$,

$$a^2 + b^2 = c^2$$
$$6^2 + 8^2 = 10^2$$
$$36 + 64 = 100$$
$$100 = 100$$

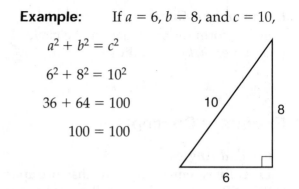

The ratio of the sides of a right triangle with angles 30°, 60°, 90° is 1, $\sqrt{3}$, 2.

The ratio of the sides of an isosceles right triangle with angles 45°, 45°, 90° is 1, 1, $\sqrt{2}$.

Circles

In the circle below, $\overline{AB}$ is the *radius* and $\overline{AC}$ is the *diameter*. The distance around the circle is the *circumference*.

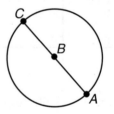

For a circle of radius r:

Circumference $= 2\pi r = \pi d$

The number of degrees of arc in a circle is 360.

Area, Perimeter, and Volume Formulas

Area of a rectangle = length × width

Area of a triangle = $\frac{1}{2}$(base × height)

Area of a trapezoid = $\frac{1}{2}(b_1 + b_2)$ height

For a circle of radius r: **Area** = πr^2

Perimeter of a rectangle = 2(length + width)

Volume of a rectangular solid =

length × width × height

Trigonometry Review for the ACT

All of the basic *trigonometric functions* are numbers (often to several decimal places) that express the ratios of two sides in a *right* triangle for one of the two smaller *angles* (10°, 45°, 89°,16.5°, x°, theta, etc.) in the right triangle.

The three sides of a triangle for trig purposes are:

1. the side *opposite* the angle in question
2. the side *adjacent* to the angle in question (other than the hypotenuse)
3. the *hypotenuse*, the longest side, the side opposite the 90° angle

In a typical example, the **sine of 45°**, or **sin 45°**, is equal to .7071. This is because the sine is the numerical value that expresses the ratio of the side *opposite* the angle to the *hypotenuse*, or in trig shorthand, *opposite over hypotenuse*. It is important to remember the word "over."

You form a *fraction* that expresses the ratio of the two sides. Often, this is all you need to do. In a right triangle with an angle of 45°, the three sides have the proportions of 1, 1, and the square root of 2. Thus the sine of 45° equals 1 *over* the square root of 2, or .7071.

Most of the work can be done using the Pythagorean Theorem ($a^2 + b^2 = c^2$) once the basic definitions are known. The ACT usually uses certain sides or angles in their items that simplify the work, such as "3, 4, 5 triangles," "5, 12, 13 triangles," "30°, 60°, 90° triangles," etc.

There are only SIX trig functions you need to know!

First, the three *simple* functions:

1. *sin* (sine) of an angle = opposite over hypotenuse (s = $\frac{o}{h}$, or **soh**)
2. *cos* (cosine) of an angle = adjacent over hypotenuse (**cah**)
3. *tan* (tangent) of an angle = opposite over adjacent (**toa**)

Start by memorizing this mystical expression:

SOH, CAH, TOA

Chant this phrase fifty or a hundred times until it is burned into your brain.

Finally, the last three functions, the *reciprocal functions*:

These functions (*cotangent, secant, cosecant*) are reciprocals of the first three. A reciprocal is a fraction with its numerator and denominator reversed.

The reciprocal of $\frac{3}{4}$ is $\frac{4}{3}$.

The three reciprocal functions can also be derived by dividing various sides of right triangles by each other, but there is a simpler way to derive them. Each is just the *reciprocal* of one of the three *simple* functions:

4. *cot* (cotangent) of an angle $= \dfrac{1}{\tan}$

5. *sec* (secant) of an angle $= \dfrac{1}{\cos}$

6. *csc* (cosecant) of an angle $= \dfrac{1}{\sin}$

It follows that if one of the simple functions equals $\dfrac{3}{5}$ or .6000, its reciprocal equals $\dfrac{5}{3}$. The

reciprocal ratio is the result, therefore, of the side that is 5 *over* the side that is 3.

Once you know the basics, you can work your way back to anything else you need to find (sides, angles, other functions, etc.) by using the Pythagorean Theorem and your knowledge of right triangles and fractions and by labeling the various sides and angles of the triangle in a drawing. Sometimes you can get the answer just by inverting a fraction, and you won't need to draw the right triangle.

All you need to remember is the information in the box below, being careful not to confuse the different functions. It would be a good idea to write them in your exam book at the first opportunity.

SOH, CAH, TOA

$$\cot = \dfrac{1}{\tan}, \sec = \dfrac{1}{\cos}, \csc = \dfrac{1}{\sin}$$

One other trig fact, concerning *radians*:

Radians are angle measures occurring at the center of a circle. A 360° angle (a full circle) has

2π (pi) radians. So any fraction of that 360° central angle, measured in radians, will be that

same fraction multiplied by 2π ($60° = \dfrac{2\pi}{6}$ radians). Remember:

360° = 2π radians

The Reading Test Competition

Description of the Test

Four passages, ten questions each. Totally ordinary. Read a passage, answer some questions. Ho hum.

The reading test is 35 minutes long.

Social Studies/Science Subscore

• One passage will cover a social studies topic.

• One passage will cover a natural sciences topic.

Arts/Humanities/Literature Subscore

• One passage will present an excerpt from a short story or novel.

• One passage will cover an area of the arts and humanities.

Total Reading Test Score

The difference between these subscores is not really meaningful. In fact, there is little validity or reliability in the subscores because a sampling of only two passages is not enough to adequately assess your ability. As far as preparation goes, your approach to each type of passage should be the same. The subscores were created to give colleges the illusion that they're getting more valuable, more detailed information.

Competitive Scoring on the Reading Test

What does it take to achieve your personal best on the ACT reading competition?

It's important for you to understand that the ACT is used for all students, not just others with reading ability similar to yours. A straight-A honors student receives the same test as a C or D student sitting across the room. The format and selection of passages is controlled by ACT. So what can YOU control?

One of your biggest points of control is to decide in advance the best number of passages for you to read. This may sound silly at first, but the majority of students can reach a higher personal score by attacking only 2 or 3 passages, instead of attempting all 4 passages.

Let's begin with a look at the impact of *ZAPPING* on one passage. The *ZAPPING* tables are based on a few assumptions:

1) If you read carefully and without rushing, you will "know for sure" between 4 and 10 answers.

2) You will blind guess or *ZAP* the unknown questions. (You should leave no blanks.)

3) The raw scores on the tables (number of problems answered correctly) reflect the average results of guessing. For example, if you blind guessed on 4 questions with a 1 out of 4 chance, your expected gain would be 2 points. In actual practice, you might pick up more or fewer points.

KNOW 4 for sure	6 UNKNOWNS on one passage		
Strategy	If Blind Guess All	If ZAP 1 Foil All	If ZAP 2 Foils All
Guess Yield	1.50	2.00	3.00
Raw Gain	5.50	6.00	7.00

KNOW 5 for sure	5 UNKNOWNS on one passage		
Strategy	If Blind Guess All	If ZAP 1 Foil All	If ZAP 2 Foils All
Guess Yield	1.25	1.67	2.50
Raw Gain	6.25	6.67	7.50

KNOW 6 for sure	4 UNKNOWNS on one passage		
Strategy	If Blind Guess All	If ZAP 1 Foil All	If ZAP 2 Foils All
Guess Yield	1.00	1.33	2.00
Raw Gain	7.00	7.33	8.00

KNOW 7 for sure	3 UNKNOWNS on one passage		
Strategy	If Blind Guess All	If ZAP 1 Foil All	If ZAP 2 Foils All
Guess Yield	0.75	1.00	1.50
Raw Gain	7.75	8.00	8.50

KNOW 8 for sure	2 UNKNOWNS on one passage		
Strategy	If Blind Guess All	If ZAP 1 Foil All	If ZAP 2 Foils All
Guess Yield	0.50	0.67	1.00
Raw Gain	8.50	8.67	9.00

KNOW 9 for sure	1 UNKNOWN on one passage		
Strategy	If Blind Guess All	If ZAP 1 Foil All	If ZAP 2 Foils All
Guess Yield	0.25	0.33	0.50
Raw Gain	9.25	9.33	9.50

For purposes of illustration, let's assume that our friend Pat knows 6 questions for sure, and blind guesses on the other 4 questions. The average pickup from guessing would be 1, so Pat's would gain 7 points from this passage (6+1).

With *ZAPPING*, however, Pat could pick up 8 points instead of 7. When multiplied by 4 passages, the reading Raw Score would climb from 28 to 32. It is clear from these tables that *ZAPPING* increases a reading score no matter where you start on the "know-for-sure" index.

How Many Passages?

Now comes the big question: How many passages should you attack? The answer depends on your natural reading speed. Every form of the ACT will present 10 questions following each of 4 passages. In an effort to complete all 4 passages in the given time of 35 minutes, many students rush much faster than they should. Because of this rushing, they often end up gaining only 4–5 points per passage.

You should not move at a speed that yields fewer than 7 out of 10 points. In other words, on every passage that you choose to attack, you need to answer 7 to 10 questions correctly. If you can't, you need to slow down.

Remember our friend Pat from the English and Math competitions? If Pat rushes through all 4 passages, the total Raw Score is between 16 and 20 points. If Pat is reading carefully, however, it's usually possible to pick up 8 to 10 points on each reading passage. The following tables show the impact of slowing down to read more carefully.

Attack 2 Passages Carefully (7 of 10), Blind Guess 2 Passages	
Gain on 20 questions careful	14
Gain on 20 questions guessing	5
Raw Score	19
ACT Score*	

Attack 3 Passages Carefully (7 of 10), Blind Guess 1 Passage	
Gain on 30 questions careful	21
Gain on 10 questions guessing	2 to 3
Raw Score	23 to 24
ACT Score*	

Attack 2 Passages Carefully (8 of 10), Blind Guess 1 Passage	
Gain on 20 questions careful	16
Gain on 20 questions guessing	5
Raw Score	21
ACT Score*	

Attack 3 Passages Carefully (8 of 10), Blind Guess 1 Passage	
Gain on 30 questions careful	24
Gain on 10 questions guessing	2 to 3
Raw Score	26 to 27
ACT Score*	

Attack 2 Passages Carefully (9 of 10), Blind Guess 1 Passage	
Gain on 20 questions careful	18
Gain on 20 questions guessing	5
Raw Score	23
ACT Score*	

Attack 3 Passages Carefully (9 of 10), Blind Guess 1 Passage	
Gain on 30 questions careful	27
Gain on 10 questions guessing	2 to 3
Raw Score	29 to 30
ACT Score*	

Attack 2 Passages Carefully (10 of 10), Blind Guess 1 Passage	
Gain on 20 questions careful	20
Gain on 20 questions guessing	5
Raw Score	25
ACT Score*	

Attack 3 Passages Carefully (10 of 10), Blind Guess 1 Passage	
Gain on 30 questions careful	30
Gain on 10 questions guessing	2 to 3
Raw Score	32 to 33
ACT Score*	

*The conversion of Raw Score to ACT Score will vary slightly depending on which form of the test you happen to take. The conversion is a statistical adjustment that makes up for the unavoidable differences in the difficulty of reading passages and questions.

Using the Program on Your Own

Use the following tips to work on your own and prepare for the ACT Reading Test.

1. **Do a reality check.**
   Complete one Reading Training Workout and determine your score using the answer key in Appendix C. As you take the test, put a star next to each question that you know for sure.

   > **Starting Score** _____

2. **Refresh your memory.**
   Study pages 64–67 in this Study Guide.

3. **Continue working on the reading passages *untimed*.**
   Take as much time as you need to read one passage at a time thoroughly, and carefully work the 10 questions that follow. You may take 10 minutes to do this, or you may need to take 20 minutes. The important thing is to take all the time you need to feel that you've done your very best.

4. **Check your answers.**
   Use the results to focus your practice on two areas: reasoning skills and pacing.

5. **Practice to improve reasoning skills.**
   With unlimited time, are you still missing a lot of the questions? Then focus your practice on reasoning skills.

   - Read the question reviews in Appendix C for all the items, not just the ones you missed. Go back and study the passage to make sure you understand why the correct answers are correct and why the wrong choices are wrong.

   - Study the wrong choices—why are they attractive? How are reading traps built into the test?

   - Look for questions where you could have applied the *ZAPPING* strategies.

6. **Practice to improve pacing.**
   Are you getting a majority of the questions correct with unlimited time? Then focus your practice on improving pacing. Some students will improve their score by focusing their efforts on only three passages instead of four. (But don't leave any blanks!) Others will improve their pacing by underlining and making notes as they read. Ask your English teacher or check your local library for other resources on improving reading speed.

   Remember, don't improve speed by sacrificing accuracy. It is more important to do well on the passages you have time for than it is to race to the end.

7. **Practice.**
   Complete the entire Reading Test in the ACT registration packet available *free* in your guidance office.

   > **Updated Score** _____

8. **Keep practicing.**
   Continue to practice, taking only one passage at a time. The Reading Test is one area where students can see a great deal of improvement with just a little bit of practice. You don't need to learn any new information; you only need to improve the skills you already possess. Go for it!

Strategies for Attacking the Reading Test

TIP 1 — Take control of the Reading competition.

During the Math Test, you took control away from the ACT by identifying the problems that were most difficult for you and either skipped them or saved them until the very end of the test.

To take control of the Reading Test, the first thing you should do is skim the passages to identify the one that appears most difficult for you personally. Write "LAST" on this passage and save it for last. If you are planning to attack only three passages, go ahead and blind guess on this "LAST" passage.

TIP 2 — Read the whole passage quickly before looking at the questions.

Do not try to memorize the whole passage. Read thoroughly but quickly and then go to the questions.

And don't stop reading near the end just because you're bored. Many students are anxious to get started on the questions, so they quit reading about halfway through the passage. BAD IDEA!

TIP 3 — Answer all ten questions after a passage before you begin reading the next passage.

- Read all four choices.
- *ZAP* if you need to.
- Guess from the leftovers.
- Do not skip any questions. No matter how confused you are by a passage, your chances of zapping and guessing correctly cannot possibly be better later on. Before you go to the next passage, make sure you have answered or guessed at each of the ten questions.

TIP 4 — Underline as you read.

- Underline the first appearance of every proper noun.
- Underline expressions that keep track of sequence, such as "initial attempt" or "in earlier periods."
- Underline words or expressions that define relationships between people or ideas.

TIP 5 Make notes in the margins.

Make notes of two to three words that capture the main point of each paragraph or important idea.

Together with underlining, making notes is a way to improve your control of the reading environment. This is not the place for passive reading. Read actively and aggressively.

TIP 6 Circle key words.

Certain key words are like road signs on the highway. They tell you which way to go and they warn you when the road is about to turn. If you miss these signs, you will get lost in your reading and may easily miss one or two questions.

Examples of Key Words

Reversal Words	Supporting Words	Result Words
on the other hand	additionally	because
however	since	so
yet	moreover	when
rather	besides	therefore
although	in fact	consequently
in spite of	furthermore	thus
nevertheless		accordingly
despite		
but		
even though		
instead		
not withstanding		

There are no absolute rules about which words to circle. The process of marking key words has three major benefits.

1. It helps you focus on the reading.

2. It helps you follow the logic of the passage.

3. It reduces the amount of time you will spend looking back for specific information.

TIP 7 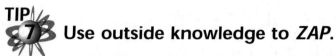 Use outside knowledge to *ZAP*.

In an actual test situation, there will be times when you read the passage and then draw a complete blank on one or more items. You may also find yourself with a time problem where you have only 3 minutes or so to read the final passage. In these cases, even without seeing the passage, you may still *ZAP* many of the reading questions.

When you can't find a specific reference in a passage, don't be afraid to use your outside knowledge. It is unlikely that the answer to any question will be factually wrong. Outside knowledge could help you *ZAP* many of the reading items.

Even when you do read the passages, use your *ZAPPING* skills to eliminate choices as you first see them, so you won't waste time re-reading choices that you know are wrong. As you go along, mark through the letters of the choices you *ZAP*.

For example, even if you did not have time to read the passage, you should be able to *ZAP* two or even three of the following choices based on your general knowledge.

> According to the passage, the Civil Rights movement in America was LEAST active during which of the following 10-year periods?
>
> **A.** the 1860s
>
> **B.** the 1920s
>
> **C.** the 1940s
>
> **D.** the 1960s

TIP 8 Use True-False clues for *ZAPPING*. Watch for giveaway words in some of the choices.

If you are having trouble solving the problem as a multiple-choice test item, think of it as four true-false questions.

Look at each choice as a true or false statement. Three statements are false—only one statement is true.

Check for words that would give away one or two of the choices as false statements.

Examples of Specific Words (usually indicate false statements)	**Example of Vague Words** (more likely to appear in true statements)
all	some
always	often
every	may
must	seem
no	most
never	usually
none	many

The following item presents an opportunity to *ZAP* on the basis of give-away words. This strategy should be applied only in situations where you don't have time to read the passage, or where you have already read the passage but it didn't make any sense to you.

Which of the following most accurately states the artist's position as implied by the first sentence of the passage?

A. Every piece of art is equally worthy of praise.

B. Art is an activity that supercedes most others.

C. All innovative art is attractive to the general public.

D. Art and society usually influence each other.

TIP 9 When time is running out, look for questions that provide line or paragraph references.

These questions can usually be answered without reading any more than a small portion of the passage.

TIP 10 Study the wrong choices offered on the Reading test in order to become aware of how the ACT editors are trying to *trap* you.

The editors at ACT do not expect you to be illiterate—they DO expect you to be careless. They build traps to catch you in your careless reading habits.

If you study the wrong choices for the reading items, you will begin to understand how they are trying to trap you. And you will learn how to avoid the traps.

The Science Reasoning Test Competition

Description of the Test

"Ordinary" is definitely NOT the word for this test. The ACT editorial staff designed and developed this test to assess your "reasoning" ability. In actual practice, it's a test of technical reading comprehension. The science you need is presented within the test itself. If it weren't for the time limit, this would probably be the favorite test of many students. It's more like a puzzle than any of the other subtests, and it could be a lot of fun for students who like a real challenge.

The test is only 35 minutes long. In that time, you need to study and understand:

- 3 data representation information sets
  (think of these problems as "graphs and charts")

- 3 research summary information sets
  (think of these as "experiments")

- 1 reading comprehension or conflicting viewpoints information set
  (think of this as "reading")

After gaining a thorough understanding of each information set, you need to answer a few questions.

- Graphs and Charts   5 items each × 3 passages = 15 items

- Experiments   6 items each × 3 passages = 18 items

- Reading Comprehension   7 items × 1 passage = 7 items

There are two features of the Science Reasoning Test that should give you a positive boost:

1. Because of the length of the test and the short administration time, most of the items require only about 30 seconds to answer. So you're not really forced to do any serious "reasoning." You need to read quickly. Many of the items require you to read all four choices and find the one that meets a certain condition. Other items are the sort where you can determine an answer from the stem, and then go looking for your answer among the choices. This doesn't mean you should be careless, just move quickly.

2. You don't need a strong science background to do well on this test. Although the various "information sets" are heavily laden with scientific information, a good reader can find most of the necessary content right in the science test. The advantage of a science background is speed and familiarity. Many choices are instantly *ZAP-able* if you have a solid background in science. However, a good performance on this test depends mostly on strategy and technical reading skills.

Competitive Scoring on the Science Reasoning Test

What does it take to achieve your personal best on the ACT science competition?

Your two main points of control on the science test are: 1) your selection of which type of passages to attack first; and 2) your allocation of time to each type of passage.

Most students find the Charts & Graphs passages easier than the others. If you spend 33 out of 35 minutes just on Charts & Graphs, your science score could still hit the national average, as illustrated below:

Use most time on CHARTS & GRAPHS Blind Guess Other 25 Questions	
Gain of 14/15 on Charts & Graphs	14
Gain of guessing on other 25 questions	6 to 7
Raw Score	20 to 21
ACT Score	

Use most time on CHARTS & GRAPHS ZAP Other 25 Questions	
Gain of 14/15 on Charts & Graphs	14
Gain of ZAPPING other 25 questions	8 to 13
Raw Score	22 to 27
ACT Score	

If you find after practice that you prefer the Experiments passages, you could hit the national average by spending nearly your entire time just on these three passages, as illustrated below:

Use most time on EXPERIMENTS Blind Guess Other 22 Questions	
Gain of 16/18 on Experiments	16
Gain of guessing on other 22 questions	5 to 6
Raw Score	21 to 22
ACT Score	

Use most time on EXPERIMENTS ZAP Other 22 Questions	
Gain of 16/18 on Experiments	16
Gain of ZAPPING other 22 questions	7 to 11
Raw Score	23 to 27
ACT Score	

Regardless of which type of passage you attack first, you need to allow as much time as you need to have confidence in every answer. Even if you require 25 minutes to carefully attack the first 3 passages, your total score will be higher than if you carelessly rush through the entire test.

The tables below represent reasonable strategies for students of various ability levels. It is not unusual even for straight-A students to run out of time on the ACT science test. The most important control issue here is for you to define your strategy in advance, and then stick to it when you take the test.

Strategy for Straight-A Student Attacking Entire Test at Manageable Pace	
Gain 14 to 15 Charts & Graphs	14 to 15
Gain 15 to 18 Experiments	15 to 18
Gain 5 to 7 Reading	5 to 7
Raw Score	34 to 40
ACT Score*	

Strategy for B+ Student Attacking Test at Strategic Pace	
Gain 14 to 15 Charts & Graphs	14 to 15
Gain 13 to 15 Experiments	13 to 15
Gain 2 to 3 Reading	2 to 3
Raw Score	29 to 33
ACT Score*	

Strategy for B Student Attacking Test at Strategic Pace	
Gain 13 to 14 Charts & Graphs	13 to 14
Gain 12 to 14 Experiments	12 to 14
Gain 2 to 3 Reading	2 to 3
Raw Score	27 to 31
ACT Score*	

Strategy for B/C Student Attacking Test at Strategic Pace	
Gain 13 to 14 Charts & Graphs	13 to 14
Gain 9 to 11 Experiments	9 to 11
Gain 2 to 3 Reading	2 to 3
Raw Score	24 to 28
ACT Score*	

*The conversion of Raw Score to ACT Score will vary slightly depending on which form of the test you happen to take. The conversion is a statistical adjustment that makes up for the unavoidable differences in the difficulty of the science passages and questions.

Using the Program on Your Own

Use the following tips to work on your own and prepare for the ACT Science Reasoning Test.

1. **Do a reality check.**
Complete one Science Training Workout and determine your score using the answer key in Appendix C. As you take the test, put a star next to each question that you know for sure.

Starting Score _____

2. **Refresh your memory.**
Study pages 74–77 in this Study Guide.

3. **Continue working only one information set (passage) at a time.**
You don't need to work an entire Training Workout at every sitting. You will get sick of it and never want to look at the ACT again. It is better to do a little bit every day over a long period than to bulldoze ahead and then quit.

4. **Don't worry about your score or about timing yourself.**
First build your skills, then work on your speed. Become familiar with the test format, the types of information sets presented, and the language and style in which the passages are written. Focus on improving your skill of reading the graphs and tables efficiently and effectively.

5. **Pay attention to the wrong choices, even on problems you got correct.**
Just like the Reading Test, there will be traps on the Science Reasoning Test. What is it about the wrong choices that makes them attractive?

6. **Study your mistakes.**
Look up each item you missed in the answer explanations in Appendix C. Why is the correct answer correct? Why are the wrong choices wrong? Are you missing more questions on one particular type of information set than on the others?

7. **Practice.**
Complete the entire Science Reasoning Test in the ACT registration packet available *free* in your guidance office.

Updated Score _____

8. **Keep practicing.**
One of the best ways to improve on the Science Test is to become more familiar with scientific writing. In the long run, you could do this by reading magazines like *Scientific American*. In the short run, just practice reading and working the ACT science passages. The more familiar you are with the actual test style, the better you will be at attacking the information sets. With a little practice, they can actually be fun!

Strategies for Attacking the Science Reasoning Test

TIP 1 Take control of the Science Test competition.

Just as with math and reading, you need to take personal control of the Science Test. There are two steps to this process.

First: Quickly write at the top of each passage "Chart," "Experiment," or "Reading." You should start your work with the passages marked "Chart."

Second: If you struggle with reading comprehension, write the word "LAST" above the reading passage. If you are a good reader, write the word "NEXT" above the reading passage.

TIP 2 Spend only about 60–90 seconds on the information set (the passage) before starting on the questions.

You will not be able to get very far on the test if you thoroughly study each information set. When you begin to attack the questions, the information set should start to make more sense. The initial need for you is to ace the first three chart passages, no matter how long it takes.

TIP 3 As you read the verbal information, transfer any notes, values, or labels to the other graphs or tables.

This exercise will help clarify the information set, and it will shorten the time that it takes to answer questions.

Do not ignore any of the verbal information presented in the passage. Read the title of each graph and table. Study the labels of the horizontal axis and of the vertical axis of every graph. Study the tables and diagrams that accompany the experimental summaries. Study the labeling and function of any components presented in a schematic diagram.

TIP 4 Use the reading tips on the Science Test.

Remember, the Science Reasoning Test is really a test of technical reading. The tips for the ACT Reading Test (pages 64 through 67) will also work on the Science Reasoning Test. Pay special attention to underlining.

TIP 5 Every problem has one and only one correct answer.

If it sometimes seems to you that two answers are correct, first double-check the question, then go back to the information set. If two choices still appear to be equal, then they are probably both wrong, since they cannot both be correct. Although the ACT editors are not infallible, the odds of you catching them with two correct answers are about zero in a million.

TIP 6 In items where all four choices need to be considered, quickly ZAP any choice that intuitively seems wrong.

Then spend time on the remaining choices. If you are unable to verify that one of these is the answer, you need to go back and reconsider the choice that you instantly *ZAPPED*. It's possible that you *ZAPPED* the right answer by accident.

TIP 7 Don't make easy questions hard.

Since you need to do so many items, some of them will be fairly easy. Look at Question 9 on page 35 of Science Workout F:

> Based on the information obtained from the experiments, which of the following would be a likely net change in the length of the zinc rod used in Experiment 1 if its length had been 25 cm?

Looking quickly at the table, we see that the zinc rod in Experiment 1 was 100 cm and it expanded .175 cm. So if it was only 25 cm, that's 1/4 of 100. The rod would expand 1/4 of .175. All we need to do is divide .175 by 4 to get the answer.

TIP 8 Be aware of the time as you move along.

When you get down to only four or five minutes, use that time to take a shot at *ZAPPING* through the remaining items. Trust your *ZAPPING* skills. If you can *ZAP* one choice out of each of the last 12 items, you should pick up 4 or 5 points even though you may not have been able to read the final two or three passages. Do not leave any blanks.

TIP 9 Many questions contain a negative twist, such as:

- Which of these <u>contradicts</u> X?

- Which of the experiments does <u>not</u> support Z?

- Which of the following discoveries <u>would weaken</u> the theory of Scientist Q?

- To which of the following would the data be <u>least</u> relevant?

- Which of these was <u>not</u> a critical factor in the experiment?

These problems must be handled carefully—and with deep concentration. It's very easy to get turned around as you consider all of the choices. When that happens, you can reach a correct conclusion, but answer the item incorrectly.

First of all, circle the negative in the item to make sure you keep it in mind as you read the choices. Then make a notation by each choice, such as "yes/no" or "y/n" or "+/−" or even "pro/con"—whatever makes sense to you. These simple notes will minimize the possibility of confusion and could save you two or three important points on the test.

TIP 10   Keep moving on this test.

You need to work at a very healthy pace to finish on time. Although you should study the passages with some intensity, do not dawdle on any of the items. If you stop and really contemplate every choice, you'll only get about halfway through the test.

TIP 11   Study the format of this test in advance.

Know what to expect before going in on the day of the real test. The directions are simple: Read the passage and answer the questions. However, it is important to study this test so that you learn to recognize the three types of passages that you need to deal with.

Study these three formats to see how they are similar and how they are different. Notice the kinds of questions that accompany each type of passage. Although the actual ACT that you take will have different topics and subject matter, the format and types of items will be the same as these. The more familiar you are, the more quickly you will be able to move through this test. This is an opportunity to gain a serious competitive advantage over students who are unprepared for the Science Test.

TIP 12   If you are sure that you won't get to finish the test, go ahead and fill in the answers to all the blanks on your answer sheet.

Then return to the point where you are working and continue to work until the time runs out. As you determine each correct answer, simply erase the previous guess. Don't let time run out while you still have three or four blank spots on your answer sheet. You could be throwing away a couple of free points. On this test, every item is worth about one ACT point.

Attacking ACT Science Graphs

On the ACT Science Test, you won't have time to thoroughly study each chart or graph. With only 60–90 seconds to spend on each "information set," it will be important for you to use your time wisely. Below are four simple steps for approaching science graphs.

STEP 1: Identify the *main idea*—the *title*.

When you see a graph on the science test, the first thing you should do is find out what it's about. Most graphs will have some sort of title. In some cases, you will need to read a paragraph to find out the subject of the graph.

STEP 2: Identify the *variables*.

- What is the horizontal variable?

- What is the vertical variable?

- Is there a third variable? Sometimes there will be. Many students miss one of the questions because they overlooked a third variable.

STEP 3: Identify the *scales*.

- Is the scale continuous or categorical?

- What are the units of measure?

- What are the minimum and maximum values on the scale(s)?

STEP 4: Read the *question*.

ACT Science questions generally fall into one of two categories:

1. Questions asking you to read or determine a value.

2. Questions asking you to understand trends and relationships.

Appendix A

Special Pages for Students Participating in a Workshop

Guessing—Case Study #1

The ACT English Test includes 75 items. What if you knew 55 answers and blindly guessed on the other 20 items? Tough Test #1 shows that, on the average, students will gain five raw score points from blind guessing on 20 items.

Case Study #1 ACT ENGLISH TEST SCORE		
	RAW SCORE	ACT SCORE
Without Guessing	55	
With Blind Guessing	60	

No matter how poorly you guess, any difference will always be in the positive direction. You can't hurt your score by guessing.

When you're guessing, do so quickly. A fast guess is just as good as a slow guess.

Tough Test

This "Tough Test" is based on the 20 hardest questions ever to appear on the ACT. These questions represent situations where most students need to guess.

Before you guess at each answer, wait for full directions from your instructor.

TOUGH TEST #2				
1	A	B	C	(D)
2	F	(G)	H	J
3	A	B	(C)	D
4	F	G	H	(J)
5	A	(B)	C	D
6	F	(G)	H	J
7	(A)	B	C	D
8	(F)	G	H	J
9	A	B	(C)	D
10	F	(G)	H	J
11	A	B	(C)	D
12	F	(G)	H	J
13	A	B	C	(D)
14	F	G	(H)	J
15	A	(B)	C	D
16	F	G	H	(J)
17	A	B	(C)	D
18	F	(G)	H	J
19	A	B	(C)	D
20	(F)	G	H	J

A

A

G
D

F
A
J

J
A
J

The Effects of Smart Guessing on the ACT

Write the number you had correct in the box below.

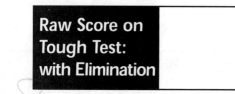

If we gave this Tough Test to a million students, the average score would be 11. If your score was higher or lower than 11, it was simply by chance.

This Tough Test clearly demonstrates that not all guessing is alike. The only difference between blind guessing and the Tough Test is that some of the choices were eliminated on the Tough Test. This helped you *zero-in* on the right answer.

On the real ACT, you can often eliminate two or even three choices.

Guessing—Case Study #2

Just like Case Study #1, let's say you knew 55 answers on the ACT English Test. You again had to guess on the other 20 items. This time, instead of blind guessing, you were able to eliminate some of the choices before guessing.

In other words, you *zeroed-in* on the answers and then picked from the leftovers. You were guessing on both tests—but on the Tough Test you were guessing between fewer choices. The average gain on the Tough Test is 11 extra points from zeroing-in before guessing.

Case Study #2 The Effects on Guessing on the ACT Test		
	RAW SCORE	**ACT SCORE**
Without Guessing	55	21
With Blind Guessing	60	23
With Eliminating Choices		

What a difference!

If you eliminate choices before you guess, you increase your odds of getting the correct answer—AND your score will go up!

Appendix B

Score Conversion Table

Estimated ACT Scores Based on Practice Test Results

Note: The tables used by ACT are slightly different for each form of the test.

Estimated ACT Score	Number Correct on English Test	Number Correct on Math Test	Number Correct on Reading Test	Number Correct on Science Test	Estimated ACT Score
36	75	60	40	40	36
35	—	—	39	39	35
34	74	59	38	38	34
33	—	58	37	37	33
32	73	57	36	36	32
31	72	56	34–35	35	31
30	71	54–55	33	34	30
29	70	52–53	32	33	29
28	69	49–51	31	32	28
27	68	47–48	30	31	27
26	66–67	44–46	29	29–30	26
25	64–65	42–43	28	28	25
24	62–63	39–41	27	26–27	24
23	59–61	37–38	26	25	23
22	57–58	35–36	25	23–24	22
21	54–56	32–34	24	22	21
20	51–53	30–31	22–23	20–21	20
19	49–50	27–29	21	19	19
18	46–48	25–26	20	17–18	18
17	43–45	22–24	19	16	17
16	40–42	20–21	18	14–15	16
15	37–39	16–19	17	13	15
14	31–36	13–15	15–16	11–12	14
13	29–30	Blind 12 Guessing	13–14	Blind 10 Guessing	13
12	26–28	10–11	12	8–9	12
11	20–25	8–9	11	7	11
10	Blind 19 Guessing	6–7	Blind 10 Guessing	6	10
9	15–18	5	9	5	9
8	13–14	4	8	4	8
7	9–12	—	6–7	3	7
6	8	3	5	—	6
5	7	—	4	2	5
4	5–6	2	3	—	4
3	4	—	2	—	3
2	1–3	1	1	1	2
1	0	0	0	0	1

99th Percentile (rows 30–36)

National Average (rows 19–21)

Estimating Your ACT Score

Step 1: Record your estimated ACT scores for one of each Training Workout. Add the ACT scores.

Test	Training Workout ACT Score
English	
Math	
Reading	
Science	
Sum of Scores	

Step 2: Use the tables below to find your estimated total ACT score.

Sum of Scores	Estimated Overall Score	Sum of Scores	Estimated Overall Score	Sum of Scores	Estimated Overall Scores
142–144	36	106–109	27	70–73	18
138–141	35	102–105	26	66–69	17
134–137	34	98–101	25	62–65	16
130–133	33	94–97	24	58–61	15
126–129	32	90–93	23	54–57	14
122–125	31	86–89	22	50–53	13
118–121	30	82–85	21	46–49	12
114–117	29	78–81	20	42–45	11
110–113	28	74–77	19	38–41	10

Appendix C

Answer Reviews

English Answer Review
Workout A

1-D   **D** is the only choice which is not redundant, since the words "must have" and "certainly" mean the same thing in this context. You should always look for such redundancies, since they often appear on the ACT.

2-G   **G** is correct because a gerund is called for. A gerund is a verb form which ends with "ing" and functions as a noun. The first use of the word "running," in "upright running" is in the gerund form. The second use must use the gerund form to remain parallel. **F** is wrong because the infinitive form "to run" is not parallel. **H** and **J** are wrong because both "it" and "the same" would seem to refer to "upright running" instead of just "running"—implying that upright running is possible on four legs.

3-B   This sentence is presented in the present tense. "Upright running is . . . and the physical structure and musculature it requires makes . . ." *ZAP* **A**, **C**, and **D** because these choices use the past tense, "required."

4-J   The sentence only makes sense if the pronoun "it" refers to the development of bipedal locomotion. Since this is unclear, good style demands that a noun such as "the change" be used in order to indicate the meaning clearly.

5-B   **A** retains the original sentence fragment. **B** creates a grammatically correct sentence. **C** creates a new sentence fragment. **D** is wrong because a sentence fragment cannot be joined to a sentence with a semicolon.

6-J   **F** and **G** can be *ZAPPED* because no punctuation is required between the words "fours" and "and." The coordinating conjunction "and" is sufficient to link the parallel words "run" and "pick up." The word "both" requires that "and" be used instead of "to," so **H** can be *ZAPPED*. You must get 5 correct to answer this correctly.

7-B   **A** and **C** are both run-on sentences. The subordinating conjunction "although" (**D**) is wrong because the two parts of the sentence it connects complement each other and should be linked with "and."

8-H   The playful tone and non-scientific observations make it clear that the author has a humorous intent in this part of the passage. It is important to identify the style and tone of passages as you read them. Expect to find a fairly wide range of narrative styles on the ACT.

9-D   The beginning of the interjected observation: "actually, he may have been the first genius" is set off from the sentence by a dash, so the end of the phrase must be followed by another dash, not a comma, to separate the entire phrase from the main sentence. Similar problems of parallelism, balance, and symmetry are sure to be on the ACT.

10-J   The phrase "on account of" (**F** and **H**) is incorrect because the preposition "of" must refer to a noun form, not a verb form like "we were destined." Notice that it is proper to say "because we were destined," but not "because of we were destined." **G** creates a sentence fragment. The only proper choice is **J**, in which the "because" idea is implied, rather than directly stated. The correct choice may leave out some of the words that are contained in the incorrectly written form of the passage.

11-D   ". . . the methods *used to bring art* to the eyes . . ." is clear, concise, and grammatically correct. Choice **A** (the form that appears in the passage), **B**, and **C** are awkward and too wordy. Phrases such as "is able to be" instead of "can be" are often reason enough to *ZAP* a choice. **A**, **B**, and **C** represent a type of wrong answer that appears often on the ACT English Test. This option type is usually longer than other choices and uses more words than are necessary to express the intended idea. Often these phrases don't sound like something people would really say. Trust your ear. If something sounds pompous or stilted to you, and the rest of the writing in the passage does not, there is a good chance that you are right and that the option should be *ZAPPED*. One trap you should look for: don't read the passage and simply choose an answer that will make the phrase in the passage work a little bit better. **B** improves **A** in this way, but both are still wrong. Be prepared to throw out the "sound" of the underlined portion of the passage and go with a different-sounding version entirely, one that attacks the problem of expressing the intended idea from a different direction. The best strategy is to *ZAP* all of the obviously wrong choices and then substitute the remaining ones for the underlined part of the passage. With practice, you will learn how ACT English questions work and the right steps to take for each item. Knowing these steps intuitively means that you can apply them fast enough to get your best score.

12-F   **F** is correct because no punctuation is needed between "press" and "to" in the sentence despite its length. Compare it to a sentence such as: "We have to work to succeed." Grammatically speaking, they are the same. It is often helpful on questions like this to make up a shortened version of a sentence with the same structure in order to simplify the problem.

13-C   Although possessive nouns use an apostrophe followed by an *s* (Frank's hat, the team's victory, the town's center), this is not the case with the pronoun *it*. The *'s* form of this pronoun is used only for the contracted form of "it is," as in "It's a beautiful day." The correct form for the possessive of *it* is "its purpose." This rule, like many rules of English grammar and usage, is not strictly logical. It is a rule that must be memorized. Several questions involving the use of an apostrophe and *s* with "it" are certain to be on the ACT.

14-F   "For example" is the best choice, since "technology" is, in fact, an "example" of the trend mentioned above. **G** suggests that what is being described is a departure from the trend, while **H** and **J** imply that it is not closely related. Questions such as this require you to make judgments about the meanings of the various possible versions of the passage. One way to recognize that this is a "meaning" question is to notice that all four choices are followed by a comma. You should know immediately from this that the question cannot be about the proper use of commas.

15-C   Questions such as this ask you to use your judgment to make a change in the passage. **C** is the best choice since it is the only one which would not add a comical or destructive image to the passage. Learn to recognize the writing style and tone that are being used in a passage. No correct choice will ever depart very far from the overall tone of the passage. Chances are good that if a choice seems a little "strange" to you, it is wrong and should be *ZAPPED*.

16-F   "World" is a singular noun. It needs to be possessive because the "museums" are "of the world," just as in "Frank's hat," the hat is "of Frank." In the possessive form of singular nouns and pronouns (with the exception of "its") the apostrophe goes before the *s*. In plural nouns it follows the *s*. (As in: "When the aliens returned to their worlds, they put the objects in their *worlds'* museums.")

17-D   **A** can be *ZAPPED* for two reasons. First, some punctuation is needed after "treasures" to indicate that it completes an independent clause (an independent clause has all the parts of a complete sentence and could stand alone as a sentence). Second, no comma is needed between "now" and "a computer." **B** and **C** can be *ZAPPED* because *both* a comma and a word such as "and" or "but" are needed to separate two independent clauses. The rule which applies is: "Independent clauses may be separated by a comma *and* a coordinating conjunction such as *and, but, for, or, yet,* etc." **D** is correct because it separates the sentence in the passage into two complete sentences.

18-G   **F** is wrong because the passage contains an obvious sentence fragment: "That are displayed anywhere in the world." **H** is wrong, because a semicolon does not belong between "paintings" and "that." A semicolon cannot be used to join a fragment to a sentence. In almost all situations on the ACT, a semicolon is only used to join related independent clauses (clauses which have all of the parts of a sentence, express a complete thought, and could stand alone). The choice here is between a dash (**J**) and no punctuation at all (**G**). The dash is wrong, because the phrase "paintings that are displayed anywhere in the world" describes what the "images," not "the paintings," are "of." Using the dash would change the intended meaning and suggest that the computer "images" are displayed throughout the world. Note that while this final choice is a difficult one to make, your chance of getting a correct answer is greatly increased by first *ZAPPING* **F** and **H**.

19-A   The two verb forms must agree. Since the passage is correct as it stands, your ear should not detect anything wrong with it and you should go on to examine the other three choices. **B** is wrong because "will look" places the looking action in the future. The action described by the verb "see" is taking place in the present, at the same time as the actions of "enlarge" and "restore." The verb "had used" places the artist in the past. **C** does take place in the present, but the word "if" makes the painter's action conditional. Therefore, the "would" form is necessary in order to make the painting's present appearance conditional as well. In the same way, **D** takes place in the past but is not conditional. Try reading the sentence with the different choices to see that it only works as it appears in the passage. Notice that "would look"—a choice that is not given—would also have worked, although it would have changed the sentence's meaning slightly.

20-H   This one should be easy if you learn to recognize a run-on sentence. A run-on sentence is two complete sentences (or two independent clauses) combined into a single sentence. The type shown in the passage (**F**) is a "fused" run-on sentence, meaning that no punctuation is used. **G** is a comma splice; a run-on sentence that uses a comma to join the two sentences. **J** is not exactly a run-on sentence, since it uses the conjunction "and" to join the two sentences. **J** is wrong, however, for two reasons. The first is that these sentences should not be joined by a conjunction, since they are not that closely related. The second is that even if the two independent clauses were closely related, joining them with a conjunction would require the use of a comma after "works." **H** separates the two sentences properly by placing a period after "works" and capitalizing the word "The."

21-D   **A** is wrong. The word "Art" is singular and "them" is plural, so the two don't agree. **B** can be *ZAPPED* for the same reason. The choice is between **C** and **D**. The ACT will often ask you to choose between a comma and a dash in situations like this. The comma (**D**) is correct here because the phrase "rather than gazing mutely at it," is initially set off from the sentence by a comma. Therefore, a comma must appear at the end for balance. If a dash preceded "rather," **C** would be correct.

22-H   This question requires you to choose the correct form for the verb "filter." By eliminating intervening words we can see that filter is part of the verb phrase "by adjusting and . . ." Only **H** works in the phrase, because, like "adjusting," it uses the "ing" ending.

23-B   **A** would keep a comma-spliced run-on sentence in the passage. **C** attempts to fix the problem, but a careful reading of the new sentence shows that it really makes no sense. Between **B** and **D**, the choice is **B**, because the word "while" correctly suggests that the two trends are merely occurring at the same time, whereas the word "since" incorrectly suggests that the first causes the second.

24-H   **F** is wrong because it would keep a comma-spliced run-on sentence and because the pronoun "it," which is singular, refers to "recording techniques," which is plural. **G** would correct the run-on sentence problem but not the pronoun problem. **H** fixes both. **J** fixes only the pronoun problem.

25-A   The question asks which sentence would effectively develop the meaning of the previous sentence. The previous sentence, after being shortened by question 13, dealt with the ability of recording techniques to alter the sound of musical performances. **A** develops this idea by suggesting that the improved techniques can actually create a second performance that can be thought of as just as "real" as the original. **B** raises the new subject of compact disc players, something that was not mentioned in the passage. **C** states that new possibilities for recording "fidelity" have occurred. This may be true, but the previous sentence dealt with the alteration of original sounds, not their faithful preservation. **D** might work if the sentence contained some proof that the recording techniques discussed were evident to a casual shopper. Since it does not, the sentence does little to develop the previous sentence and raises new questions which it does not answer.

26-G   This question requires that you use your ear to eliminate sentences that are awkward or contain errors. **F** is awkward because the word "first" is located in an odd position. Did Schnitger tap his cane somewhere else later? Did other people tap their canes later? Did Schnitger tap on the floor with something other than his cane later? Also, the sentence implies that Schnitger used only one technique, cane-tapping, to plan the organ. **G**, on the other hand, makes a simple statement which tells what Schnitger did and how the activity was related to organ-planning. **G** should be left un-*ZAPPED* and the next two choices should be read to see if they work. **H** is constructed oddly and uses more commas than it ought to. **J** is no better than **H**. Notice how it uses "first" next to "planning." Of course you plan first. You don't need to say both.

27-C   The details of Paragraph 3 support the central idea of Paragraph 4. References to "a large cathedral" and "an intimate night club" are examples of changing the "character of the sounds." Paragraph 3 should, therefore, follow Paragraph 4.

28-G   If you read the passage carefully, you should realize that the author deliberately avoids expressing an opinion. This should allow you to *ZAP* **F** and **J**, the two "yes" choices. **H** can be *ZAPPED* because the passage does mention various kinds of art. The correct "no" answer is **G**, because the task described could have been easily completed without discussing the various kinds of electronic art, but the failure to express any opinion at all on the central issue clearly falls short of the assignment.

29-B   No punctuation is necessary after "humans."

30-G   Since an idea very similar to this one has already been clearly stated in the expression "Almost since the beginning of time," the entire phrase is unnecessary.

31-C   The main idea of the first paragraph is the wide range of useful products produced for and by humans from bulrushes. **C** gives actual examples of two famous bulrush products, and would be interesting to most readers. It is the choice which best fits the criteria given in the question. Vivid examples are often the best choices for questions such as these.

32-J   A colon is needed to link the statement to the words "sewage treatment." The statement implies that it will be directly followed by the name or names of the thing that it is discussing, a situation that requires a colon. None of the other forms of punctuation, or lack of punctuation, would work here.

33-D   A, B, and C are all awkward for a number of reasons. The word "discovered" is preferable to the longer form "made the discovery" even without the various complications that this usage creates in the other three choices. **D** is the shortest and simplest choice.

34-J   "Containing" is shorter and more direct than "in which there are" (**G**). **F** is clearly awkward. **H** uses the phrase "polluted by . . . pollutants" which is redundant.

35-D   The word "currently" means "right now" and calls for the present tense, so **A** and **B** can be *ZAPPED*. **C** can be *ZAPPED* since commas are not necessary to set off an adverb placed between a verb form such as "are trying."

36-H   Breaking this long, complicated, and grammatically-flawed sentence into two parts is clearly the best choice in terms of style. When a choice on the ACT is two shortened sentences that retain the intended meaning and are grammatically correct, it is usually the best choice.

37-C   When faced with a question like this, it is necessary to consider the style, tone, and content of the passage as a whole. In this case, the lack of any serious technical details eliminates **A**. **D** can also be eliminated, although at first glance it appears attractive. The passage is not so much simplifying technical issues, but providing general background information. **B** is wrong since the tone of the passage is not a plea, and the theme of environmental pollution, while touched on, is not a strong motivating factor to the writer. The writing style and content are more like those you would find in a piece of light journalism. Under these circumstances, **C** is the best choice.

English Answer Review
Workout B

1-B   The words "widely" and "by many" both modify the verb "believed" and communicate the same idea. When both are used the sentence is redundant. **B** is the only choice that eliminates one of the words.

2-F   **F** uses the verb "to declare" correctly. There is no reason for the comma in **B**, and the words "to be," "as," and "is" are all unnecessary and examples of poor diction. When the shortest answer to an ACT English item seems correct, it is usually the best choice.

3-C   One "nation" is being spoken of, so the singular form of the possessive is called for.

4-J   The rule of parallelism applies here. The nouns in the series "law," "commerce," and "government" call for a fourth singular noun to be used to complete the sentence.

5-C   The simplest choice is the best. All of the others are unnecessarily complicated.

6-F   **G** and **H** are too wordy and introduce unnecessary clauses into the sentence. **J** is wrong because the meaning is made somewhat unclear by separating "call" and "for independence." **F** is another example of "shorter is better."

7-C   A pair of commas is needed to set off the explanatory phrase "where the local dialect is essentially a separate language" from the main clause. **C** and **B** are the only choices that include the first of these two commas. **B** is wrong because the phrase "which is" is unnecessary.

8-F   The first part of the paragraph deals with distrust and resentments that have arisen from language differences. To reinforce this theme the sentence would have to give further evidence of this phenomenon. **F** is the only choice which does this.

9-A   "Bring about" is the only one of the four choices which means "cause." It is clear from the rest of the sentence that this is the meaning which is intended.

10-H   Two contradictory ideas are suggested by this portion of the passage and a word such as "however" is needed to show the proper relationship between them.

11-D   The subject of "suggests" is the noun "examination," which is a singular noun. **C** and **D** are the only choices which give the correct form of the verb. **C** is wrong because no comma is necessary.

12-J   **J** states the intended meaning of the sentence in the clearest form. Each of the other sentences has problems with usage, sentence structure, and word choice.

13-B   The original passage contains a sentence fragment. It is an introductory clause, and should be separated from the sentence which follows it by a comma.

14-F   The subject of the sentence should be a plural pronoun referring to the words "immigrant groups." "Their" is the only correct choice for such a pronoun.

15-C   **C** is the best choice from a stylistic viewpoint. It is the only option which is not awkward and wordy. It states the intended idea completely and fully. Read each of the other choices to yourself and notice the ways in which they are awkward and unclear. With practice, you should be able to *ZAP* each of them quickly and go on to the next question without spending much time.

16-G   The "point" made by the previous sentence concerns the enrichment of the English language by the addition of foreign words and phrases. **F** and **G** both deal with the subject of foreign languages being brought to America, but **G** is best because it gives actual examples of the phenomenon. **H** and **J** introduce new subjects rather than reinforce the earlier sentence's point.

17-B The passage as it stands contains a comma-spliced run-on sentence. Two complete sentences convey the clearest expression of the intended meaning, as in **B**. **C** and **D** attempt to eliminate the run-on sentence by creating subordinate clauses, but the meaning of the sentence is unclear in both cases.

18-F To reinforce the view that the threat of language diversity should not be taken seriously, any addition should deal specifically with the subject and offer some evidence that concerns are unwarranted. **F** cites similar concerns in the past and shows that they were unreasonable. Using historical evidence to make a point about the present is a valid, persuasive device and would work very well in this case. **G**, **H**, and **J** do not deal directly with the issue of feeling threatened by other languages.

19-A A colon should be used at the end of a complete sentence to indicate that clarifying information will follow. This is true of the passage as it stands. The comma (**B**) does not work here; it seems to leave the concluding phrase hanging without a clear sense of its relationship to the rest of the sentence. The addition of the word "in" (**C**) does not improve **B**, and actually makes it worse because it lengthens the concluding phrase for no reason and repeats the word "in." The word "namely" (**D**) accomplishes the same thing as a colon, but is more colloquial in tone and clashes with the serious tone of the rest of the passage. In addition, changing the word "place" to "places" has made it unacceptable, since it still must agree with the singular article "a."

20-J **F** is wrong because a comma is needed to set off the introductory phrase from the main clause. **G** is wrong because the present tense is used to describe an event in the past. **H**, however, uses the correct tense, and the choice is between **H** and **J**. **J**, which creates an introductory phrase separated by a comma, is shorter, less awkward, and it conforms to standard usage.

21-B No comma is necessary between "planters" and the phrase describing the planters, so **A** and **D** are wrong. The word "who" is used correctly, while "such as were" is a wordy example of non-standard usage. Once again, the shortest gramatically-correct expression is the best one.

22-J "Emigrate from" and "leave" refer to the same noun and have the same meaning, so only one is needed. *ZAP* **F**, **G**, and **H**. The only choice which eliminates this redundancy is **J**.

23-D This item requires you to take into account the comma after Ulster. You're not free to eliminate this comma. Therefore, **B** and **C** would ruin the sentence. *ZAP* them. Your choice is between **A** and **D**. **A** is awkward. *ZAP* it.

24-J **F** is wrong because it is unclear who "they" are. **G** and **H** are awkward. **J** is the shortest and clearest answer.

25-B The previous sentence states that the Scots in Ulster were isolated from other groups. A description of this isolation (**B**) would be the best way to strengthen this point.

26-G As used here, the words "intolerable" and "unbearable" have the same meaning. Their function is to suggest that the Scots wanted to leave Ulster, and either word would be sufficient for this purpose. **G** is the only choice that eliminates the redundancy.

27-C **A** leaves a sentence fragment in the passage. **B** is wrong because a comma is necessary to separate the main clause from the adverbial clause. As you read the sentence, you can hear a natural pause after "left." **C** uses the comma correctly. **D** incorrectly uses a semicolon. A semicolon will not work where a period won't work.

28-J **F** is wrong because the paragraph at this point is primarily about the heavy Scottish migration to Philadelphia, not the English settlers who were already there. **G** also develops the wrong idea, Philadelphia's development, as does **H**. **J** is the best choice since it provides interesting modern day evidence of the Scottish migration during the period discussed.

29-C   **A** is a comma-spliced run-on sentence. **B** looks all right, but it is no better than **D**. Both can't be right, so **B** and **D** can be *ZAPPED*. **C** is a correctly punctuated compound sentence. No comma is necessary in **D**, and the word "therefore" is unnecessary since the idea is clearly implied by the rest of the sentence.

30-F   No punctuation is required between "dialect" and "sustained." All of the other choices create sentence fragments and are clearly wrong.

31-A   **A** states the idea simply and is correctly punctuated. The commas used to set off "and the oral tradition" are wrong in **B**. **C** uses a plural verb form ("lives") where a singular form ("live") should be used. **D** is a tempting choice, but it is not as good as **A** because it uses extra words and punctuation for no apparent reason.

32-G   You should learn the meanings of the easily-confused *their, they're,* and *there. Their* is the possessive form of "they," so **G** and **J** are the only possible correct choices. The extra words "those who are" in **J** are unnecessary, making **G** correct.

33-C   A singular possessive form is called for. **C** is the only choice that has the proper ending.

34-F   **F** is the shortest and best answer. **G** uses "like" with a verb form where "as" should be used. **H** introduces the noun "it" without a verb to accompany it. **J** gives "it" the passive verb form "is believed to be," but the expression is awkward and confusing compared to **F**.

35-A   **A** is a simple and clear way to state the intended idea. **B** and **C** use the pronoun "you," but it is not clear who "you" refers to. **D** is awkward and wordy.

36-H   No comma is called for so **G** and **J** can be *ZAPPED*. A careful reading of the sentence indicates that the action took place in the past, so the form "would have been" should be used instead of "will have been."

37-A   No comma is needed between "ballads" and "sung." The past participial phrase "sung in the Scottish lowlands in the days of James I" acts as an adjective, modifying the noun "ballads." The formation is no different grammatically than the expression "bicycle built for two." Therefore, **B** and **D** can be *ZAPPED*. The past participle of "sing" is sung. Therefore, **A** is the correct choice.

38-G   Paragraph 2 is the chapter in which the frontier life of the Scots-Irish is described, and therefore, it is the best place to discuss their reputations as Indian-fighters. Paragraph 1 is mostly about their origins in Europe and paragraph 3 is about their modern descendants. A new paragraph at the end would disrupt the chronology of the passage.

English Answer Review
Workout C

1-B   Subject-verb agreement. The subject *distinctions* is plural so the verb *was* needs to change to *were*. No commas are needed, so *ZAP* **C** and **D**.

2-G   Parallel verb forms. *To build shelter* is a task along with *gathering food* and *making clothing,* so the verbs *gathering, to build*, and *making* are parallel and all should be in the same form. *To build* should be *building*.

3-D   *Usually in most cases* is redundant. **D** is the only answer which corrects this redundancy.

4-F   No change. Although the underlined portion seems long, none of the answers improve on this, and each introduces a punctuation error.

5-C   A sentence fragment precedes the period. Although the fragment is disguised as a long group of words, your clue is the word *with* at the beginning of the sentence.

6-H   Faulty parallel. The words *creation* and *correcting* carry equal weight in the sentence and should be parallel in form and case. Since both belong to *problem*, they must have the singular possessive case: *Its creation* and *problem's solution*.

7-D   Shorter is usually better, and in this case, you should delete the whole portion. The words *which should be avoided whenever possible* are obvious and therefore add nothing new about the ideas of *greed for profits, prevalent disease, widespread suffering,* and *poverty*.

8-H   Subject-verb agreement. The subject *culture*, which follows the verb *were*, is singular; therefore, *were* should change to its singular form, *was*.

9-A   Shorter is usually better. No change is required since all three choices would make the original longer than it needs to be.

10-G   Punctuating a nonrestrictive phrase. The phrase *with their nimble fingers and small size* is a nonrestrictive modifier that should be set off with commas. (A nonrestrictive modifier is not vital to the meaning of a sentence.) Looking ahead of the underlined portion, you should have noticed a comma. A single comma will never come between a subject (*children*) and its verb (*were*), so a comma is necessary between *children* and *with*.

11-B   A sentence fragment follows the underlined period, so **A** (NO CHANGE) can be *ZAPPED*. **C** can also be *ZAPPED* because a semicolon, like a period, only connects complete sentences. (If a period won't work, neither will a semicolon.) **B** and **D** both correct the fragment, but **D** is longer than necessary.

12-J   *Bad* and *inadequate* are redundant. Only **J** corrects this redundancy.

13-D   Awkward writing. Two phrases in a row are introduced with *which*, making the sentence sound clumsy. **B** creates a sentence fragment. **C** removes a comma instead of correcting the real problem. **D** removes the first *which*.

14-G   Subject-verb agreement. The pronoun *some* can take a plural or singular verb, depending on what it refers to. Here, it is plural, referring to some of the factory owners. (Compare *Some of this banana is bruised* to *Some of these bananas are bruised*.)

15-B   Shorter is better. Although the phrase *where the problem usually tended to be greater than it was in agricultural countries* seems to say a lot, it doesn't add any new information and therefore should be deleted.

16-J   Whole-passage question. You must read each choice and decide if it is true or false. **F** states that the writer's opinion is so strong that the writer may be disregarding fact or reason in favor of his or her opinion. If so, a reader won't know what to believe. This is not true, for the issue of child labor is well known and the author's opinion isn't unique. *ZAP* **F**. Also, since this issue is well known, it would be easy to find facts to support the passage. *ZAP* **G**. **H** says that opinions should never be stated in an essay without support. There can be exceptions to this. When a choice on the ACT uses words like "never," "always," and "everybody," there is a good chance that choice is wrong. *ZAP* **H**. **J** is a gentle critique, calling for just a few specific details. **J** is reasonable.

17-A   Whole-passage question. The passage gives general information about child labor practices. It doesn't argue against these practices, as though it were persuading people against child labor (**B**). It is too general for a college course (**C**), and it has little to offer for someone trying to protect children today (**D**).

18-G   *Its* is a possessive pronoun for *America*, not to be confused with *it's*, which is a contraction of *it is*.

19-A   Verb tense. The verb form *could grow* is consistent with the tense of the paragraph. See the following verbs from the first three sentences; your ear should tell you they go together: first sentence, *has held*; second sentence, *could grow*; third sentence *have faced*.

20-F   Previous-sentence box question. **F** is a concrete example of what the first sentence says. As a general rule, you should always try to support a statement with undisputed facts. The first sentence here says that America has promised that anyone could grow up to be whatever he or she wanted. The second sentence states a common belief that the presidency is not beyond anyone's reach (**F**)—an indisputable example of what is meant in the first sentence. **G** says what is already said in the second sentence. **H** is unrelated. **J** is too general.

21-C   Antecedent-pronoun agreement. When a pronoun is underlined, you should check for its antecedent. The antecedent for *it* is *advantages of education or geographical mobility*. This antecedent requires that you use the plural pronoun, *them*, and that it be correctly punctuated within a nonrestrictive modifier. A nonrestrictive modifier can be separated from the sentence by a pair of commas or a pair of dashes, but not both.

22-H   Shorter is usually better. The word *in* is not needed in the underlined portion.

23-B   Previous-sentence box question. The previous sentence says our parents and grandparents usually accepted the jobs that came their way. To demonstrate the reality of this, the writer should cite concrete examples. **B** gives the reader examples: farm, market, dock, and factory work.

24-H   A fragment follows the period. Since question 39 does not correct the fragment, it depends upon question 38 to do so. **G** is wrong; if a period doesn't work, neither will a semicolon. **J** is wrong; the colon won't work because the following sentence is not an example of what is stated before the colon.

25-C   Antecedent-pronoun agreement. The pronoun refers to *parents* and *grandparents* three lines earlier. *Their* is the correct plural possessive pronoun.

26-J   The comma splits the predicate and should be removed. This sentence is similar to *I'm glad that you are here*. A comma wouldn't work after the verb *glad*.

27-A   No change. Answer foils **B** and **D** invite you to incorrectly change the tense of the verb. **C** and **D** tempt you by introducing a semicolon, which would create a sentence fragment.

28-G   Previous-sentence box question. Expanding an idea is easily accomplished by citing concrete examples. *Vocational counselors, job fairs, books on career changing* are examples that elaborate on the previous sentence's mention of *endless number of careers*.

29-D   Run-on sentence, or a comma splice. A comma incorrectly used to connect two clauses. Since the two sentences must be properly separated, you can *ZAP* **A** and **B**. Although *yet* can be used to connect two sentences, it does not correctly describe the relationship between the two clauses. *Yet* implies contrast. **D** is correct because the colon demonstrates that the words *when we are free to choose . . . circumstances* are an example of *the blessing is clear*. Note that this must be solved with question 44.

30-G   The comma between *choose* and *life's work* makes the sentence more clear. Otherwise, a reader may think that the author means to say *when we are free to choose our life's work*, instead of *when we are free to choose, our life's work does not have to be . . .* The semicolon will not work, for the first clause is not complete (**H**). **J** is a workable choice, but since it achieves the same affect as **G**, the word *Then* is unnecessary.

31-A   Diction. This question is inviting you to replace *for example* with a different phrase. This isn't necessary because the surrounding sentence is an example, or clarification, of the *darker side* mentioned in the previous sentence.

32-J   Whole-paragraph question. It is important to view all of the answer foils before choosing an answer. Only **J** suggests not beginning a new paragraph, while **G** and **H** are really no better than **F**. When a phrase says *the result being*, it is probably the result of something said in the previous paragraph, and should be included in that paragraph.

33-D   You'll run into many situations like this when you take the ACT. The writing is simply not very good. About all you can do is *ZAP* both **A** and **B** and then decide whether nothing is better than "providing." *. . . and a source of . . . satisfaction as well as a hefty income.* Since it works OK to omit the underlined portion, the answer is **D**.

34-H   Run-on sentence. **H** is the only choice that separates the two sentences.

35-A   Paragraph 3 presents an idea that contrasts with the central point of Paragraph 2. Paragraph 4 draws a conclusion regarding the contrast. Paragraph 3 should therefore remain where it is.

English Answer Review
Workout D

1-D   A sentence fragment follows the period. **A** and **B** will leave a fragment. **C** and **D** will correct the fragment, but only **D** will preserve the parallel structure. *Result of pure chance* is grammatically parallel to *lucky event* and must be placed in a parallel position within the sentence. Your ear should tell you that **C** is incorrect.

2-F   No change. A long introductory phrase is usually set off by a comma. As you read the sentence, you should feel a natural pause after *story*.

3-C   Verb form. The author is using the passive voice: *Fleming was presented*. The passive voice tells the reader what has happened (*presented with the miracle of penicillin*) and to whom (*Fleming*). Fleming wasn't doing the presenting; rather he was being presented with something.

4-F   Possessive case. For most nouns, the singular possessive is formed by adding an *'s*. A possessive noun does not have to be a person's name.

5-C   Whole-passage question. As a general rule, essays present an idea and support it with examples. Often one paragraph states an idea and supports it with examples called supporting sentences. Explaining the discovery of penicillin will take several paragraphs. This is acceptable because the main idea is still being supported by examples.

6-F   Punctuating nonrestrictive modifiers. The words *a man who . . . years* is an appositional statement that modifies Fleming. Since this kind of modifier restates what was said previously, it is a nonrestrictive modifier and should be set off with commas, or one comma if it is at the end of the sentence.

7-A   Concreteness. The previous sentence alludes to background information about Fleming. A sentence about his scientific interests as a student would be a logical addition to the background information.

8-G   Parallel structure. A comma is not needed between items with parallel status within a clause. *Isolating* and *identifying* are parallel. This is like the sentence *Apples and oranges are my favorite fruits*. You wouldn't put a comma after *apples* or *oranges*.

9-A   Punctuating nonrestrictive modifiers. This must be solved with 72; in fact, it may be easier to do 72 first. With the underlined words of 72 removed, this phrase is an appositional statement that modifies *battle*. Since this modifier is vital to the sentence, it should be separated with a comma and not made into its own sentence (**C** and **D**).

10-J   Shorter is usually better. The comment about World War I adds no useful information to the sentence.

11-D   Shorter is usually better. *Possessed of the capabilities* means the same thing as *was able to*.

12-G   Whole-passage question. The passage's main point is to get the reader to reconsider the story of penicillin's discovery: not that it was pure luck, as is often believed, but a result of Fleming's skill, insight, and fortune. An audience of science teachers would already know this (**F**). If the audience were ignorant of Fleming (**H**), the author wouldn't have to dispel the myth. There is no point presenting an argument to scientists who already know the argument (**J**); such a group would want to hear something new.

13-B   Whole-passage question. The quotation referred to is an example of what the author meant when he or she said that Fleming's discovery was luck or pure chance. As a general rule, examples should follow general statements.

14-G   The sentence contains two verbs: "concerns" and "has led." One of them has to be removed. Changing "concerns" to "concerning" makes the phrase "concerning the existence of life under very hostile conditions" a modifier of "discovery."

15-D   Redundancy. "Wonder" and "ask themselves" are redundant. Only **D** eliminates the redundancy.

16-J   Shorter is better. The phrase "quite like any other known microbe" doesn't need to be introduced with "which is" (**F**) or "that is" (**G**). **H** changes the meaning of the sentence by suggesting that the bacteria which was recently found lived a long time ago. Another clue that the sentence is flawed is in the comma following "Bacteria." There should be two commas or none. Since you can not insert another comma after "microbe," **J** solves the problem by allowing you to remove the comma.

17-C   Sentence fragment. A sentence fragment follows the period, so **A** and **B** won't work (a semicolon cannot replace a period). **C** is correct because a comma is not needed after "found." The sentence is similar to "I found my keys by looking under the table." You would not need a comma after "keys."

18-H   Subject-verb agreement. The subject is "water temperature" and the correct verb is "was recorded." Answer **J** tempts you with a shorter option, but careful reading will show that you cannot omit the verb.

19-C   When possible, sentences should be followed with examples that capture the reader's interest. **A**, **B**, and **D** are things a textbook would list. Since this is an essay, it needs to be more interesting than a textbook. **C** has a gory appeal that may interest a reader; in addition, it develops the idea in the previous sentence.

20-F   The sentence is correct. **G** and **H** prompt you to make a punctuation error. **J** introduces a subtle inaccuracy: the bacteria do not thrive without needing the benefit of light; they thrive without the benefit of light. In addition, "there" reminds the reader that the bacteria are from the deep ocean.

21-D   The verb "have gave" is incorrect. Removing "have" corrects the grammar without changing the sentence. **B** and **C** create redundancies ("earlier" is redundant with "previous" and "once").

22-F   The complete idea is "thought to be drawn." This is the way the sentence should be written. To omit the words "to be" (**J**) leaves the sentence a little vague. Shorter is only better when no meaning is lost.

23-A   Phrases beginning with "which" are often separated by a comma. "That" and "which" often can be used interchangeably, which is your clue that **B** and **C** are unacceptable. If you chose **B** or **C** you would be saying that the black smoke bacteria leaks sulphurous gases. **D** would create a sentence fragment.

24-J   The sentence is redundant with the previous sentence. Notice that the previous sentence says "Scientists are looking with interest for answers to some of life's mysteries . . ." Every other choice is awkward.

25-C   The first sentence of the passage mentions the "possibility of life on other planets." It is appropriate for an essay to return to an idea that was referred to in the beginning.

26-J   Shorter is usually better. Only **J** gets to the point without loss of detail.

27-B   The reader does not know who "they" refers to, so you can *ZAP* **A**. **C** is too long. **D** changes the meaning of the sentence by implying that the gland's powers are called "the master gland." **B** eliminates the problem by restating the phrase in passive voice—"it is called."

28-H The sentence following the period is a fragment, and so is the solution offered in **J**. **G** would create a run-on sentence. **H** correctly connects the fragment to the previous sentence.

29-D If you omit the words between the subject and the verb, you will see that the subject is "one," which doesn't correspond to the verbs "are" or "were." **C** changes present tense to past tense, which is unnecessary.

30-F The sentence is correct. **G** invites you to use long and cumbersome language. **H** and **J** invite you to incorrectly use the possessive case. The possessive of "it" is "its," not to be confused with "it's" (it is).

31-B The phrase "which is an abnormal state" is redundant. We know that giantism is an abnormal state, so the phrase is unnecessary.

32-H The words "But wouldn't you know" are too informal. Compare a textbook with a letter from a friend. The letter might have phrases like "wouldn't you know," but a textbook would not. This essay is written more like a textbook, so informal language should be removed.

33-C The underlined words have two problems: 1) they create a run-on sentence, and 2) they are redundant. The comma should be followed by a conjunction like "and." The "most" is redundant with "smallest." **C** corrects the run-on sentence and removes "most."

34-J The sentence says three things were made by the finest craftsman: clothing, shoes, and furniture. A list of three items should be punctuated as shown in this explanation. Since these three items are a subject for the verb "made," you would not put a comma after "furniture."

35-A The words "such as arthritis" are an example of "uncomfortable symptoms." This type of modifier is set off with commas. Choices **B** and **C** create sentence fragments.

36-H The essay is addressing hormone diseases, and only **H** makes it clear that the diseases that are becoming less common are growth hormone diseases.

37-D Shorter is better. Any technique that humans use to produce a growth hormone will be a synthetic technique. In using the shorter version (**D**) you also remove a redundancy.

38-F The phrase "While this enables doctors to help prevent dwarfism" is correctly punctuated. This question is trying to get you to introduce a punctuation error.

39-D The singular verb needs to be plural. "Pituitary glands and growth rates" is the compound subject for the verb "is." The correct form should be "are." **B** will not work because "remains" is also in the singular form. **C** changes the meaning.

40-J An essay should focus on one topic and stay on the subject. The paragraph of the two famous dwarfs is largely unrelated to the topic of diseases and treatments related to the growth hormone.

English Answer Review
Workout E

1-D Punctuation. The phrase *about two of the ocean's better known inhabitants* is crucial to the meaning of *confusion*. Without the phrase, the reader would not know what the confusion is, so this phrase should not be separated from the word *confusion* by a comma. The semicolon in **B** creates a sentence fragment. **C** separates deal from confusion, which is no better than the original.

2-G Verb tense. Since the paragraph is in the present tense, the present tense form, *represent*, is appropriate.

3-A The underlined portion is correct as is. **B** creates a fragment, because a semicolon can only join two complete clauses. **C** creates a fragment by separating the phrase from its sentence. **D** uses the word "including" twice, making the sentence awkward.

4-H Whole-paragraph question. The first two sentences prompt the reader to wonder what the difference between dolphins and porpoises is. The third sentence gives an answer based on their scientific classification.

5-D The phrase *their family name is phocaenidae* is a nonrestrictive modifier. Such a modifier must be set off with dashes or commas. Either could be used and a choice between these would be unfair, but **D** is the only one that uses the same punctuation before and after the clause.

6-J Shorter is usually better. The commentary *which is . . . weighed* is unnecessary and should be deleted. Choice **G**, creates a sentence fragment; **H** misuses commas as the original does.

7-A No change. **B** and **C** would create a sentence fragment. **D** would separate *that dazzles us* from *creature*.

8-G A sentence fragment follows the period after *whale*, and in this case, the fragment adds no worthwhile information. The sentence is better with it left out.

9-B Diction. **C** and **D** make the sentence longer than necessary. The difference between **A** and **B** is in the choice of preposition, *on* or *of*. *Of* sounds better.

10-H Diction. *Answer, issue,* or *problem* do not make sense in the sentence. *Distinction* does, because it implies something you would use to separate the two species. Note that the word *difference* is in the following line.

11-B Subject-verb agreement. The subject is *difference*, although it is easy to assume that *two* is the subject. *Difference* is singular, requiring *is* instead of *are*.

12-H Whole-passage question. The passage implies that it is going to tell us how to tell the two species apart, but then fails to do so. This is the weakness of the passage, which could be corrected by some explanation of the distinction between the two species.

13-A Correct as is. The question is tempting you to change the punctuation when no change is necessary.

14-F This is a good place to use *ZAPPING*. *ZAP* **H** because it's too wordy. *ZAP* **J** because you don't capitalize the word following a semicolon. The only difference between **F** and **G** is the insertion of the word *is*. It's unnecessary. Remember, when you get down to two choices and they both look good to you, shorter is better. *ZAP* **G**.

15-C Sentence fragment. A sentence fragment follows the period. Since *homes* and *historic sites* are parallel, they should be joined by *and* rather than with a comma.

16-J Diction. This sentence contrasts a *desirable place to live and work* and the *richest and most interesting places in America for a family vacation*. The words *not only* best prepare the reader for this contrast.

17-C Pronouns. The correct form of the reflexive pronoun is *themselves*. This sentence is similar to *I can help myself*. You would not say *I can help me*.

18-J Shorter is usually better, and in this case, it is the only phrase that will not sound clumsy.

19-D Shorter is usually better. The comparison to Los Angeles is unnecessary and should be omitted.

20-G *Early* and *original* are redundant. Only **G** deletes one of these words.

21-D Diction. Since more than two sites are alluded to (*Betsy Ross's house, Christ Church, Independence Hall*, and the *Liberty Bell*), *best* should be used instead of *better*, which reduces the choices to **C** and **D**. **D** offers the shortest version.

22-H Sentence fragment. A fragment follows the period. A colon won't connect the two parts because *near the Delaware River and its docks* is not an example of the *east side of town* (**G**). A semicolon won't work because it can only join complete clauses (**J**).

23-A Possessive pronouns. *Its* is the correct possessive pronoun for *Delaware River* and should not be confused with *it's*, which means *it is*.

24-G Punctuating nonrestrictive modifiers. This problem should be solved with 60. The phrase *a time when European sailing ships were loaded there with agricultural and forest products* is appositional and should be set off with commas.

25-D *From upriver* is part of the appositional phrase *a time when European sailing ships were loaded there with agricultural and forest products*, which modifies *three hundred years ago*. It should not be separated from the rest of the phrase.

26-H The first thing to decide on this type of question is which paragraph should come first. Obviously not #3, so *ZAP* **J**. Which paragraph seems more "introductory," #2 or #1? This is a close call, but #2 is better. *ZAP* **F**. Now the choice is whether #3 or #1 should come next. It's not perfectly clear why, but #1 should follow #2, and #3 should be last.

27-A Whole-paragraph question. Paragraph 3 deals with Philadelphia's history (**A**), not architecture (**B**), Penn's design (**C**), or the muddy river bank (**D**).

28-G The second and third sentences need to be connected, otherwise they make no sense. How could it be a "certainty" that railroads could make a town rich when the owners often changed their minds or went bankrupt? The word "but" should be used to set up this contrast. **H** and **J** do not.

29-A The current possessive form is correct. The merchants are "of the town." You could say "town merchants" (**D**), but you would have to keep the comma. **D** removes the comma.

30-H If you omit the portion between the dashes, the sentence reads, "The town's merchants, fearing that Thatcherton was going to get Hopkinville's railroad." This is a sentence fragment, so *ZAP* **F**. You can *ZAP* **G** because the subject—the town's merchants—has already been stated, and does not have to be restated with "they." **J** is incorrect because a semicolon can only separate two independent clauses, and the first part of the sentence is a dependent clause. **H** is the most reasonable answer.

31-A The verb tense is correct as is. **B** is definitely wrong because "could of" is an incorrect way of saying "could have." **C** and **D** force an incorrect tense.

32-J Whole-paragraph question. **F** is not correct, for little emphasis is put on the writer's grandfather. **G** and **H** are not correct, because the first paragraph answers these questions. **J** is correct, because we don't know why the railroad barely made its deadline.

33-C   The words "So that" make the sentence following the period a run-on sentence. **B** also creates a run-on sentence. For **D** to be correct, it would require a comma between "night" and "and."

34-G   Two sentences are incorrectly connected with "and." If the two sentences were closely related, a comma would go before "and," but since they are not, they should be two separate sentences with no conjunctions (and, but, so, or) between them.

35-B   This question asks you to think about the writer's tone. The author intends to be slightly humorous and noncommittal about certain parts of the celebration. The reader should not take everything the author is saying literally.

36-F   The author has demonstrated a slightly humorous tone in the previous paragraph. **F** would continue this sense of humor by implying that no one has celebrated in Hopkinville for the 120 years after this party. We can deduce that the author is making fun of the present day Hopkinville.

37-A   Simple writing is best. Answers **B** and **D** invite you to use complicated punctuation for no apparent reason, and **C** creates a sentence fragment: ". . . but when I close my eyes, as she did when she was alive" is an incomplete clause.

38-J   A sentence fragment follows the period. **G** is too long. **H** uses a semicolon incorrectly.

39-A   "Their father's" is the correct form of the possessive since more than one boy is sitting on the shoulders of more than one father.

40-G   "decked out in their finest dresses" modifies "ladies of Hopkinville." This kind of modifier is preceded by a comma, a symbol for a natural pause. Omitting the underlined portion would remove a vivid description.

41-B   If you look through the essay, you will see that it is about a single person's thoughts. Notice that the first and fourth paragraphs begin with the word "my." It is important to be aware of the style of an ACT passage. This is a very personal essay so the writer isn't limited to formal beginnings and closings.

English Answer Review
Workout F

1-A The sentence is correct. "Administering medicines" occurs in the present and "requires" is the correct present-tense form of the verb.

2-J The phrase beginning with "your good judgment but . . ." needs to better imply the contrast between "good judgment" and "ability to relate to children as people." The word "but" is your clue that the sentence is awkward. "Both" (**G**) does not support this contrast. "More than your" (**H**) sounds good but changes the meaning. It would imply that your ability to relate to children as people is a greater asset than your good judgment. Whether this is true or not, the author did not mean to say this, so by choosing **J** the author's meaning is preserved.

3-A Since "of course" can be removed from the sentence without any loss, it should be set off with commas.

4-G If you read just the subject and verb, the sentence says "a young person will be resisting taking medicine." The verb is "will be resisting taking," which sounds awkward. "Will resist taking medicine" sounds more natural.

5-D Shorter is better. Rarely does a writer need to say "thing." Choices **A**, **B**, and **C** retain the wordiness of the original sentence.

6-F This is the correct form of the possessive. "One" refers to a person. "One's manner" is like saying "a person's manner."

7-C Answer **C** is the most specific statement. It gives the reader the most clear image of what the writer means by saying "manner, words, and tone of voice should all convey a positive attitude."

8-H Look at the skeleton of the sentence. The simplest form of the sentence says ". . . you should respond to questions." Looking at it this way, you should see that only "with truthfulness" (**H**) adequately completes the sentence.

9-D The words ". . . will to some extent grow . . ." mean as much as ". . . will grow . . ." so "to some extent" can be deleted. **B** and **C** achieve the same affect as "to some extent."

10-J Your clue that the sentence can be improved is that "Or" and "however" are in the same sentence. Paragraph breaks are intended to put a piece of writing into bite-size pieces for the reader. Inserting a new paragraph here is logical because the discussion is changing from distasteful medicine to pleasant tasting medicine.

11-D The sentence has two verbs where it only needs one: "are" (in the contraction "They're") and "can be." Only **D** removes one of the extra verbs.

12-H The introductory phrase is "For very young children." This type of phrase is set off with a comma. Possessives are not the issue (**F** and **J**). Semicolons don't set off phrases that aren't complete clauses (**G**).

13-B "Secretly" and "camouflage strategies" are redundant and inserting a period creates a fragment. Only **B** corrects the redundancy and correctly connects the two parts of the sentence. Notice that even though a comma doesn't have to precede "but" in this sentence, writers often use one to emphasize the contrast.

14-G Shorter is better. All the answers mean the same thing, but **G** uses fewer words.

15-A   The question invites you to change the punctuation around the modifier "even those who show a great deal of resistance." Since this modifier ends with a comma, it should begin with a comma.

16-H   Whole-passage question. You are being asked to describe the author's audience in writing this essay. The content suggests that it is not for someone who often administers medicine. This rules out doctors and nurses. **J** can be ruled out because the passage makes no special mention of how to deal with children in a hospital.

17-B   Run-on sentence. The comma between "principal" and "he" creates a run-on sentence spliced by a comma. It is important to recognize that the phrase "refused to allow . . ." is critically describing the principal in question. The semicolon (**D**) is not the best choice because it will separate "principal" from "refused to allow . . ." Both "who" (**B**) and "that" (**C**) will connect the phrase but "who" is correct because the phrase refers to a person.

18-F   The sentence is correct. The answer choices invite you to change the verb form (**G** and **J**) or insert commas between the subject and verb (**H** and **J**).

19-C   The paragraph speaks of the principal's objections in the past tense: "Motivating him were . . . ," "he believed . . . ," and "he feared . . ." The verb feel should be in the past tense: "felt."

20-F   This is the correct form of the plural possessive, since there is more than one student involved. **G** makes the sentence wordy. **H** and **J** are incorrect possessives.

21-C   The antecedent of "they" is unclear. "They" refers to "the articles" but since a reader can mistake "they" to mean people, it is preferable to be more exact.

22-G   You can best understand the principal's motivation through his words or actions, rather than imagining his probable reactions to the situations described in **F**, **H**, and **J**. **G** is the only answer that directly refers to the principal's actions.

23-D   As written the sentence contains a run-on sentence spliced by a comma. The phrase following the comma contains "which," making the phrase too dependent on the preceding words, so **B** and **C** won't work. **D** removes the comma, creating a complete and smooth phrase: "in agreement with a lower court which had previously ruled in favor of the students."

24-H   This sentence contains a dangling modifier. The sentence begins with "Arguing that the student newspaper . . . ," but the subject is "the newspaper." The sentence means that the newspaper is arguing that the student newspaper is a public forum. This is not true. The lower court argued that it was a public forum. Only **H** uses the correct subject.

25-A   The sentence is correct. This sentence is similar to "I thought that you were right." You would not put a comma after "thought."

26-G   The phrase beginning with "That students in American public schools . . ." can be introduced with a colon or a dash. Whether to use a dash or colon is the writer's choice, so the ACT will not force you to choose between a dash or colon unless both are wrong answers.

27-B   The correct way to finish this sentence is to say "adults do" or "adults." Only one of these is offered as an answer. Notice that two of the incorrect answers (**C** and **D**) tempt you to use different but still incorrect possessive forms.

28-F   The paragraph is explaining how the court decided that students have rights as adults. When arguing a point or illustrating an example, essays cite facts and examples. **F** is an example that fits in with how the court views students' rights.

29-C   The sentence is incorrect as written, because the comma after "then" is not needed. The words "in fact" and "therefore" also followed by commas are no better than "then," for they mean the same thing. "However" is a word that sets up a contrast. The viewpoint of saying "no" in this paragraph is being contrasted with saying "yes" in the previous paragraph. "However" strengthens this contrast and is always separated with commas.

30-J   This is a question that comes up often on the ACT. There is nothing really wrong with any of the choices. You simply have to use your ear to pick the right response.

31-C   To choose the correct word, you need to read the whole sentence. The word "charting" was used. One charts a course, not an attitude, view, or viewpoint.

32-G   As it is written, the sentence refers to "the Court" as "they," which is incorrect. **H** is incorrect because "they're" means "they are." **J** is incorrect because "it's" means "it is." **G** is correct; implicit in "the belief" is the knowledge that the belief is "the Court's."

33-B   Whole-passage question. Sentence 4 is a general statement. Sentence 1 speaks of the courts' more conservative view, and sentence 4 says what was underlying this view. Both sentences are a prelude to the more specific descriptions in sentences 2 and 3.

34-G   The first two paragraphs say, "Imagine that you are a member of the Supreme Court" and "the case reached you for a decision." Saying that "your decision will have lasting consequences . . ." encourages you to take the task more seriously, so you will read paragraphs 3 and 4 more carefully.

Math Answer Review
Workout A

1-C Fred owns one more book than the average of the other three. The average of the other three is their sum divided by 3.

$$\frac{22 + 17 + 24}{3} = \frac{63}{3} = 21$$

Remember, Fred has one more so he has $21 + 1 = 22$.

2-J To find the decimal value of $\frac{20}{19}$ divide 20 by 19.

```
        1.05
   19)20
       19
        1 00
          95
           5
```

The closest answer is 1.05. If you have no idea how to start this problem, *ZAP* **F** and **G** because they are less than 1. *ZAP* **K** because it is almost 2.

3-D The perimeter of a square is 4 times the length of a side or $4x$. The area of a square is the length of a side squared or x^2. You are told in the problem that the area is $4x + 12$ so you can set $4x + 12$ equal to x^2.

$x^2 = 4x + 12$

$x^2 - 4x - 12 = 0$ Subtract $4x$ and 12 from each side.

$(x - 6)(x + 2) = 0$ Factor.

$x - 6 = 0$ or $x + 2 = 0$

$x = 6$ or $x = -2$ The length of the side can't be negative so 6 is the length of the side.

The perimeter is $4 \cdot 6$ or 24.

4-G The question asks for the length of the motor boat. Since the yacht is 40 feet longer than the motor boat, if you add 40 to the length of the motor boat it will equal the length of the yacht.

$$(m + 5) + 40 = 2m^2$$

$$m + 45 = 2m^2$$

Since this is a quadratic equation, subtract terms from both sides to get an equation with zero on one side and then factor.

$$2m^2 - m - 45 = 0$$

$$(2m + 9)(m - 5) = 0$$

$$2m + 9 = 0 \text{ or } m - 5 = 0$$

$$m = \frac{-9}{2} \text{ or } m = 5$$

The length must be positive so $m = 5$. The length of the motor boat is $m + 5$.

5-B The two right triangles are congruent by the Hypotenuse-Leg theorem. $\angle CAB$ has the same measure as $\angle DCA$ because they are corresponding parts of congruent triangles. Since $\angle DCA$ and $\angle ACE$ make a straight line they add up to 180°. $\angle DCA = 180° - 131° = 49°$ so the measure of $\angle CAB$ is 49°.

6-G This problem expects you to know $\sin^2 \theta + \cos^2 \theta = 1$.

$$\frac{1}{\sin^2 \theta + \cos^2 \theta} = \frac{1}{1} = 1$$

7-B Let r = radius of the circle. The rectangle has a length of $2r$ and a width of r. The area is 18, so you can solve for r.

$$(2r)(r) = 18$$

$$2r^2 = 18 \qquad \text{Divide by 2.}$$

$$r^2 = 9 \qquad \text{Take the square root.}$$

$$r = 3$$

The area of a circle is πr^2. Substitute $r = 3$.

$$A = \pi(3)^2$$

$$A = 9\pi$$

8-J   To find out how much the customers will pay, first find out how many baseballs were sold. Divide the total profit of $17.00 by the profit on each of $0.85 to find out how many baseballs were sold.

$$\begin{array}{r} 20. \\ .85\overline{)17.00} \\ \underline{17.00} \\ 00 \end{array}$$

If the customers buy 20 baseballs at $4.50 each, the total amount they will pay is $20 \times 4.50 = \$90$.

9-B   Jane is paid $110x$ for the first 110 subscriptions. She still needs to be paid for the other 5 subscriptions to be paid for all 115. She is paid $5 \bullet 2x = 10x$ for those 5 subscriptions since she is paid twice as much for each of them. Altogether she is paid $110x + 10x = 120x$.

10-H x more than m is $m + x$.

x less than $2m$ is $2m - x$.

To get the product multiply:

$$(m + x)(2m - x)$$

$$= 2m^2 - mx + 2mx - x^2 \quad \text{Add the middle terms.}$$

$$= 2m^2 + mx - x^2$$

11-A   If segment AB is inside the circle, then it must be shorter than the diameter. The diameter is the distance all the way across the circle through the center and is twice the radius. The radius is 2 so the diameter is 4. $AB < 4$.

12-H   To find out how many flowers 5 people can make in 10 hours, first find out how many they can make in 1 hour, then multiply that number times 10.

In 1 hour: $\dfrac{100 \text{ flowers}}{8 \text{ people}} = \dfrac{x}{5 \text{ people}}$

$8x = 500$

$x = \dfrac{500}{8}$ or 62.5

In 10 hours: $62.5 \bullet 10 = 625$ flowers.

13-A $\overline{BC}$ is the side opposite $\angle A$ and $\overline{AB}$ is the hypotenuse. The sin function uses those two sides.

$\sin = \dfrac{\text{opposite}}{\text{hypotenuse}}$ Substitute 10 for the hypotenuse, 0.669 for the sin 42°, and $\overline{BC}$ for the side opposite.

$0.669 = \dfrac{BC}{10}$ Multiply by 10.

$\overline{BC} = 6.69$

Note: The hypotenuse of a right triangle is the longest side so you can *ZAP* **D** and **E**.

14-H The area of a triangle is one half of the base times the height. If you use side $\overline{CB}$ as the base, then $\overline{AC}$ is the height. $\overline{CB}$ is y units long and you can use the Pythagorean Theorem to find $\overline{AC}$.

$$(\overline{AC})^2 = x^2 - y^2$$

$$\overline{AC} = \sqrt{x^2 - y^2}$$

$$\text{Area} = \frac{1}{2}y\sqrt{x^2 - y^2} \text{ or } \frac{y}{2}\sqrt{x^2 - y^2}$$

15-A The area of a triangle is one half of the base times the height. In this problem the base is $2a - b$ and the height is $2a + 2b$ so:

$\text{Area} = \frac{1}{2}(2a - b)(2a + 2b)$	Foil the two factors.
$= \frac{1}{2}(4a^2 + 4ab - 2ab - 2b^2)$	Combine the middle terms.
$= \frac{1}{2}(4a^2 + 2ab - 2b^2)$	Multiply by $\frac{1}{2}$.
$= 2a^2 + ab - b^2$	

16-J $84 = 2 \times 42$ but 42 is not prime so factor it.

$84 = 2 \times 6 \times 7$ but 6 is not prime so factor it.

$84 = 2 \times 2 \times 3 \times 7$ Now all factors are prime.

You can *ZAP* **A**, **B**, and **C** because the answers contain numbers that are not prime.

17-A

$i(2i + 9) = x - i$	Multiply by the i.
$2i^2 + 9i = x - i$	Add i to each side.
$2i^2 + 10i = x$	Replace i^2 with -1.
$2(-1) + 10i = x$	Multiply by the 2.
$-2 + 10i = x$	Rearrange the terms.
$10i - 2 = x$	

18-J Subtract 2 from both sides of the equation to get $5x^2 + 3x - 2 = 0$. Substitute $a = 5$, $b = 3$, and $c = -2$.

$$b^2 - 4ac = 3^2 - 4(5)(-2)$$

$$= 9 + 40$$

$$= 49$$

Since $x > 20$, there are 4 values less than 25 that can equal x. {21, 22, 23, 24}.

19-B   Since the choices are so close together, you can't tell which choice is correct by looking at the graph. By using intercepts $(0, 6)$ and $(5, 0)$ you can find the equation of the line.

The slope $= \dfrac{6 - 0}{0 - 5} = \dfrac{-6}{5}$ so the equation in slope intercept form is $y = \dfrac{-6}{5}x + b$.

To solve for b, substitute the coordinate pair $(0, 6)$ for (x, y).

$$y = \frac{-6}{5}x + b$$

$$6 = \frac{-6}{5}(0) + b$$

$$6 = b$$

The equation is $y = \dfrac{-6}{5}x + 6$.

Substitute 2 for x and p for y to find the correct value of p.

$$p = \frac{-6}{5}(2) + 6$$

$$p = \frac{12}{5} + 6$$

$$p = \frac{-12}{5} + \frac{30}{5}$$

$$p = \frac{18}{5}$$

$$p = 3\frac{3}{5}$$

20-G   The slopes of two perpendicular lines are negative reciprocals. The equation of line

$q\left(y = \dfrac{3}{2}x + 2\right)$ is given in slope intercept form. The slope of line q is $\dfrac{3}{2}$ and the slope of line k

is $\dfrac{-2}{3}$. In slope intercept form, line k has the equation $y = \dfrac{-2}{3}x + b$ where b is the y-intercept. To

find b, substitute the point $(2, 2)$ into the equation and solve for b.

$$2 = \frac{-2}{3}(2) + b$$

$$2 = \frac{-4}{3} + b$$

$$2 + \frac{4}{3} = b$$

$$\frac{6}{3} + \frac{4}{3} = b$$

$$b = \frac{10}{3}$$

Math Answer Review
Workout B

1-D   You can simplify what is inside the parentheses first. Remember that when you multiply powers of the same base, you add the exponents.

$$(3y \bullet 4y^2 \bullet y^3)^2 = (12y^6)^2$$

$$= (12y^6)(12y^6)$$

$$= 144y^{12}$$

2-J   Remember to look at the choices to see the format that you need for the answer. To solve x follow these steps:

$$3x - 1 = 4 \qquad\qquad \text{Add 1 to both sides of the equation.}$$

$$3x = 4 + 1 \qquad\qquad \text{Now divide each side by 3.}$$

$$x = \frac{4 + 1}{3}$$

3-B   Since $\triangle ABC$ is a right triangle, use the Pythagorean Theorem to solve for side $\overline{CB}$:

$$(AC)^2 + (CB)^2 = (AB)^2$$

$$(4)^2 + (CB)^2 = (8)^2 \qquad\qquad \text{Square.}$$

$$16 + (CB)^2 = 64 \qquad\qquad \text{Subtract 16.}$$

$$(CB)^2 = 48 \qquad\qquad \text{Take square root.}$$

$$(CB) = \sqrt{48} \qquad\qquad \text{Simplify.}$$

$$(CB) = \sqrt{16} \bullet \sqrt{3}$$

$$(CB) = 4 \bullet \sqrt{3}$$

4-J   The center of the circle is the midpoint of the diameter. To find the midpoint of $\overline{AB}$, find the average of the x-coordinates and the average of the y-coordinates.

$$\left(\frac{-1 + 3}{2}, \frac{5 + 5}{2}\right) = \left(\frac{2}{2}, \frac{10}{2}\right) = (1, 5)$$

Note: You could also plot the points given as choices on the graph. Since both A and B are on the horizontal line $y = 5$, the y-coordinate of the center must also be 5. You can *ZAP* **G** and **H**. Since **K** has the same coordinates as A, you can *ZAP* **K**.

5-A Since the greater answer must be greater for all numbers $x > 1$, you just need to pick any number greater than 1 and substitute it in each equation. The greatest number will be the correct answer. Set $x = 2$.

  F. $\frac{2+1}{2-1} = \frac{3}{1} = 3$

  G. $\frac{2-1}{2+1} = \frac{1}{3}$

  H. $\frac{2}{2+1} = \frac{2}{3}$

  J. $\frac{2}{2-1} = 2$

  K. $\frac{2-1}{2} = \frac{1}{2}$

  $\frac{x+1}{x-1}$ will have the greater value for all $x > 1$.

6-H There are four geometry facts that you need to know to work this problem.

One angle of the triangle measures 90° because this is a right triangle. The measures of the other two angles add up to 90° because the sum of the measures of all the angles of a triangle must be 180°. Each of those two angles measures 45° because in an isosceles triangle at least two angles have equal measures. That means that $\angle PRQ$ has a measure of 45°. $\angle PRS$ has a measure of $180 - 45 = 135$ because together those two angles form a line.

7-A The large numbers in this problem make it hard to factor or use the quadratic formula. Subtract 22 from both sides to get an equation with zero on one side by itself.

  $6y^2 + 29y - 22 = 0$ Factor.

  $(3y - 2)(2y + 11) = 0$

  $3y - 2 = 0$ or $2y + 11 = 0$ Solve each equation for y.

  $3y = 2$ or $2y = -11$

  $y = \frac{2}{3}$ or $y = \frac{-11}{2}$

The only answer given in the choices is $\frac{2}{3}$.

8-G To get $|f(-3)|$ substitute -3 in for a in the equation $f(a) = a^2 + 4a$ and take the absolute value of the answer.

  $|f(-3)| = |(-3)^2 + 4(-3)|$

  $= |9 - 12|$

  $= |-3|$

  $= 3$

9-A The question asks for the sum of the measures of $\angle ABE$ and $\angle DCE$. $\angle DCE$ has the same measure as $\angle ABE$ because when two parallel lines are cut by a transversal then alternate interior angles are congruent. $\angle AEB$ measures 40° because together with $\angle DEB$ they make a line. $\angle EAB$ measures 90°. $\angle ABE$ measures $180° - 90° - 40° = 50°$ because the sum of the measures of the three angles of a triangle is 180°. Since $\angle DCE$ has the same measure as $\angle ABE$ they each measure 50° and their sum is 100°.

10-J Look at the format of the choices given. To get the expression in that form, factor it. The greatest common factor of the two terms is $4xy^2$. Factoring $4xy^2$ out of the $8x^2y^2$ leaves $2x$ and factoring $4xy^2$ out of $-4xy^3$ leaves $-y$. So the correct factorization is $4xy^2(2x - y)$.

Note: You could find the correct choice by multiplying each of the choices together to see which one matches the expression $8x^2y^2 - 4xy^3$ from the question. If you did that the correct products are:

    A. $4xy(2xy - 2y^2) = 8x^2y^2 - 8xy^2$

    B. $4x^2y^2(2 - y) = 8x^2y^2 - 4x^2y^3$

    C. $4xy(2x - y) = 8x^2y - 4xy^2$

    D. $4xy^2(2x - y) = 8x^2y^2 - 4xy^3$

    E. $2xy^2(4x - 2) = 8x^2y^2 - 4xy^2$

11-A $x - \dfrac{7x}{3} > 1$ Multiply both sides by 3. Combine the x terms.

     $3x - 7x > -3$ Divide by -4.

     $-4x > -3$

     $x < \dfrac{3}{4}$ Reverse the inequality sign.

12-J To find the third side of a right triangle, use the Pythagorean Theorem $a^2 + b^2 = c^2$ where c is the length of the hypotenuse and a and b are the lengths of the two legs.

     $2^2 + 4^2 = c^2$

     $4 + 16 = c^2$

     $20 = c^2$

     $\sqrt{20} = c^2$ Remember that to simplify a radical you need to factor it to bring out factors that are perfect squares.

     $\sqrt{2^2 \bullet 5} = c$

     $2\sqrt{5} = c$

13-B Substitute $p = 3.1$, $q = 4.6$ and $s = 3.5$ into the equation:

     $\dfrac{p + q}{r} = 25$

     $\dfrac{3.1 + 4.6}{r} = 2(3.5)$ Do the multiplication and addition with the numbers.

     $7.7 = 7r$

     $1.1 = r$

14-J   Translate the words in the problem into an equation and solve for x. x is the number of pencils in the box. "Multiply x by 5 and decrease the result by 8" is the expression $5x - 8$. "3 times a number which is 2 greater than x" is the expression $3(x + 2)$. The problem says that the two expressions are equal.

$5x - 8 = 3(x + 2)$ Simplify.

$5x - 8 = 3x + 6$ Add 8 to both sides.

$5x = 3x + 14$ Subtract $3x$ from both sides.

$2x = 14$ Divide by 2.

$x = 7$

15-E $4x^2 - 3x - 1 = 0$ is a quadratic equation and can be solved by factoring.

$4x^2 - 3x - 1 = 0$

$(4x + 1)(x - 1) = 0$

$4x + 1 = 0$ or $x - 1 = 0$

$4x = -1$ or $x = 1$

$x = \dfrac{-1}{4}$

The solution set is $\left(\dfrac{-1}{4}, 1\right)$.

16-F   By looking at the choices, you can see that the format is the same as the solutions that come from the quadratic formula.

$$x = \frac{-b \pm \sqrt{b^2 - 4ac}}{2a}$$

The only difference between the two answers given by the quadratic formula is the plus or minus sign in the numerator. The solution given in the problem is $\dfrac{-3 + \sqrt{2}}{2}$ so the other one must be $\dfrac{-3 - \sqrt{2}}{2}$.

17-C   The question asks for the area of the triangle. Since the base is given in terms of the height and the height is given in terms of the base, the height (h) and the base (b) can be found with two equations. The two equations are $b = h - 4.5$ and $h = 2b + 1$. If you substitute what h is equal to in the second equation into the first equation, you can find b.

$b = (2b + 1) - 4.5$

$b = 2b - 3.5$

$b = 3.5$

Now substitute 3.5 in for b in the second equation to find h.

$h = 2(3.5) + 1$

$h = 7 + 1$

$h = 8$

The area of a triangle equals $\frac{1}{2}bh$.

$\frac{1}{2}(3.5)(8) = 14$.

18-G   The question says that one angle of a triangle measures $x°$ and asks for the sum of the other two angles. Since the sum of all three angles of a triangle equals 180°, the sum of the remaining two angles is $(180 - x)°$.

19-A   Since the two triangles are similar, the measure of $\angle DEC$ equals the measure of $\angle BAC$. $\angle ABF$ and $\angle ABC$ form a line so the measure of $\angle ABC$ is $180° - 120° = 60°$. The sum of the measures of the angles in a triangle is 180°. So $\angle BAC = 180° - 90° - 60° = 30°$. Since $\angle DEC$ has the same measure, the answer is 30°.

20-K   Neither of the first two choices simplify and neither of them is equal to y^{27} so simplify the last 3 choices.

H. $(9y)^3 = 9^3 \cdot y^3 = 729y^3$

J. $(y^9)^2 = y^{18}$ (Remember that you multiply exponents when you have a power to a power.)

K. $(y^9)^3 = y^{27}$

MathAnswer Review
Workout C

1-D 40% of the 50 members support the tax increase. To find out how many members that is, multiply .40 times 50.

.40 × 50 = 20

80% of this group of 20 members believe the increase will pass. To find out how many members are in this group, multiply .80 times 20.

.80 × 20 = 16

2-F Since $\triangle ACE$ is an equilateral triangle, each angle measures 60°. An altitude drawn to each opposite side from points E and A create two 30°, 60°, 90° triangles. Since we know that the sides of the triangles are equal and that the angles are congruent, the ratio of the areas is 1:1.

3-A $4a + 4 = 11$ Subtract 4.

$4a = 11 - 4$ Divide by 4.

$a = \frac{11 - 4}{4}$

4-K To solve the inequality, follow these steps:

$4x + 7 < -17$ Subtract 7 from each side.

$4x < -24$ Divide each side by 4.

$x < -6$

5-C How far apart the point is from the y-axis is determined by how far the x-coordinate (or first coordinate) is from zero. Point A is 3 units away. Points B, D, and E are each 2 units away. Point C is only 1 unit away.

6-J The formula for the circumference of a circle is $C = 2\pi r$. In this problem, $16 = 2\pi r$, so $8 = \pi r$

and $r = \frac{8}{\pi}$.

7-E To solve an equation with a radical in it, first get the radical on one side of the equation by itself.

$$\sqrt{x-5} - x = -5$$ Add x to each side.

$$\sqrt{x-5} = x - 5$$ Square each side.

$$x - 5 = x^2 - 10x + 25$$ Subtract to get zero on one side.

$$x^2 - 11x + 30 = 0$$ Factor.

$$(x-6)(x-5) = 0$$

$$x - 6 = 0 \text{ or } x - 5 = 0$$

$$x = 6 \text{ or } x = 5$$

6 is the only answer given.

Note: The correct choice to this question can also be found by plugging the choices in for x. The only one that doesn't yield a negative under the radical is 6.

8-G The $\cot \theta = \dfrac{1}{\tan \theta}$ so the $\cot \theta = \dfrac{1}{\frac{12}{5}} = \dfrac{5}{12}$.

9-B If the ratio of boys to girls is $x{:}9$, then there is some number, (n), that allows you to take x times n to get the number of boys and 9 times n to get the number of girls. The total of the boys plus the girls must equal 500.

$$xn = \text{number of boys}$$

$$9n = \text{number of girls}$$

$$xn + 9n = 500$$ Now solve for n in terms of x.

$$(x + 9)n = 500$$

$$n = \frac{500}{x + 9}$$

The question asks for the number of girls.

$$9n$$

$$= 9\left(\frac{500}{x+9}\right) \text{ which is the same as } 500\left(\frac{9}{x+9}\right).$$

10-F To find the equation of a line through two points first find the slope. The slope equals the change in y divided by the change in x.

$$\frac{6-1}{1-(-4)} = \frac{5}{5} = 1$$ Use the point $(1, 6)$ and the slope to simplify the equation.

$$y - y_1 = m(x - x_1)$$

$$y - 6 = 1(x - 1)$$

$$y - 6 = x - 1$$

$$y - x = 5$$

11-A   One of the numbers is $x + 2$ and the other is $x - 3$. The sum is $x + 2 + x - 3$ or $2x - 1$. The problem says that the sum is 11 so $2x - 1 = 11$ is the correct equation.

12-K

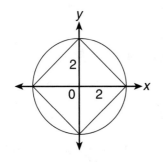

Draw a picture to see what the square looks like. To find the perimeter, you first need to find the length of a side of the square. To find the length of a side, use one of the right triangles and the Pythagorean Theorem. The hypotenuse of the triangle will be the length of one side of the square. The side of the square $= \sqrt{2^2 + 2^2} = \sqrt{4 + 4} = \sqrt{8} = 2\sqrt{2}$. Since the perimeter is four times the length of a side, $4(2\sqrt{2}) = 8\sqrt{2}$.

13-E   To find the intersection of two lines, multiply one equation by some number so that when you add the other equation (or some multiple of it) one of the variables drop out.
$-2(2x + y = -1) = -4x - 2y = 2$. Add the two equations.

$$3x + 2y = -2$$

$$+ \frac{-4x - 2y = 2}{-x = 0} \text{ or } x = 0$$

Plug 0 in for x in one of the equations.

$$2(0) + y = -1 \text{ or } y = -1$$

Note: You could find the correct choice by plugging each point into one equation. If it doesn't work, *ZAP* it and if it does, plug it into the other equation because it must work in both.

14-G

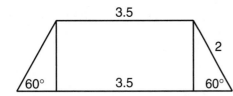

Since both base angles are the same, the two legs of the trapezoid are both 2. To find the length of the longer base, draw to the base to make a rectangle and two $30° - 60° - 90°$ triangles. In a $30° - 60° - 90°$ triangle, the short leg is one half of the hypotenuse. Since the hypotenuse is 2, the short leg is 1. The long base of the trapezoid is $3.5 + 1 + 1 = 5.5$. The perimeter of the trapezoid is $5.5 + 2 + 2 + 3.5 = 13$.

15-B   If you multiply each choice by $x(8^2)$ to get $16x$, then $16x$ divided by $x(8^2)$ will equal the choice.

$$\frac{16x}{x(8^2)} = \frac{16x}{x(64)} = \frac{16x}{64x} = \frac{1}{4}$$

16-H Since the problem gives you the sin $x = \frac{1}{3}$ and asks for the cos x, you can use the identity:

$$\sin^2 x + \cos^2 x = 1$$

$\frac{1^2}{3} + \cos^2 x = 1$ Square $\frac{1}{3}$.

$\frac{1}{9} + \cos^2 x = 1$ Subtract $\frac{1}{9}$.

$\cos^2 x = \frac{8}{9}$ Take the square root of each side.

$\cos x = \frac{\sqrt{8}}{\sqrt{9}}$ Substitute 3 for $\sqrt{9}$.

$\cos x = \frac{\sqrt{8}}{3}$

17-E $(-3)^2 - (-2)^2 = 9 - 4 = 5$

18-H $x > \frac{1}{2}x + 10$

$\frac{1}{2}x > 10$

$x > 20$

Since $x > 20$, there are 4 values less than 25 that can equal x. {21, 22, 23, 24}.

19-B The ratios mean that for every 4 apples there is 1 orange and that for every 4 apples there are 7 peaches. That means that for every 1 orange there are 7 peaches and the ratio of oranges to peaches is 1:7.

20-J A and B each have a y-coordinate of 4. Since $\overline{AB}$ is a diameter, the center of the circle is on the same horizontal line $y = 4$ and has a y-coordinate of 4. The distance between A and B is the diameter of the circle. The diameter is equal to 5 and the radius is one half the diameter or 2.5. The point on the circle with the largest y-coordinate is straight up from the center, a distance of 2.5. The y-coordinate of the point asked for is $4 + 2.5 = 6.5$.

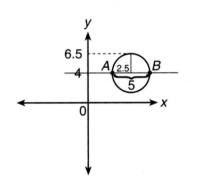

Math Answer Review
Workout D

1-B   Translate the words in the problem into an equation and then solve for x. One side of the equation is separated from the other by the phrase "the result is." The left side says x is multiplied by 4 and divided by 5 $\left(\dfrac{4x}{5}\right)$. 30 less than x is $x - 30$. 21 greater than that number is $(x - 30) + 21$. Now write the equation and solve for x.

$\dfrac{4x}{5} = (x - 30) + 21$ Add 21 and -30.

$\dfrac{4x}{5} = x - 9$ Multiply both sides by 5.

$4x = 5x - 45$ Subtract $5x$ from both sides.

$-1x = -45$ Multiply both sides by -1.

$x = 45$

2-H   Since $a = b$, replace b with a in each equation and simplify both sides to see if they match.

F. $(\sqrt{a + b})^2 = 2a^2$

$(\sqrt{a + a})^2 = 2a^2$

$(\sqrt{2a})^2 = 2a^2$

$2a = 2a^2$

Not True

G. $\sqrt{a} \bullet \sqrt{b} = \dfrac{b}{a}$

$\sqrt{a} \bullet \sqrt{a} = \dfrac{a}{a}$

$\sqrt{a^2} = 1$

$a = 1$

Not True

H. $\dfrac{\sqrt{(a)^b}}{\sqrt{(b)^a}} = \dfrac{a}{b}$

$\dfrac{\sqrt{a^a}}{\sqrt{a^a}} = \dfrac{a}{a}$

$1 = 1$

True

J. $\dfrac{1}{\sqrt{a}} \bullet \dfrac{1}{\sqrt{b}} = \dfrac{1}{2ab}$

$\dfrac{1}{\sqrt{a}} \bullet \dfrac{1}{\sqrt{a}} = \dfrac{1}{2a \bullet a}$

$\dfrac{1}{\sqrt{a^2}} = \dfrac{1}{2a^2}$

$\dfrac{1}{a} = \dfrac{1}{2a^2}$

Not True

K. $\sqrt{ab} \cdot \sqrt{ab} = ab^2$

$$\sqrt{a \cdot a} \cdot \sqrt{a \cdot a} = a \cdot a^2$$

$$\sqrt{a^2} \cdot \sqrt{a^2} = a^3$$

$$a \cdot a = a^3$$

$$a^2 = a^3$$

Not True

3-B To solve a quadratic equation, set the equation equal to zero and factor.

$11x - 2x^2 = 5$	Add $2x^2$ to both sides.
$11x = 2x^2 + 5$	Subtract $11x$ from both sides.
$0 = 2x^2 - 11x + 5$	
or $2x^2 - 11x + 5 = 0$	Factor.
$(2x - 1)(x - 5) = 0$	
$2x - 1 = 0$ or $x - 5 = 0$	
$2x = 1$	
$x = \frac{1}{2}$ or $x = 5$	

4-K To find miles per hour, divide miles by hour.

$$\frac{14r^2 + 21rs}{7r} = \frac{7r(2r + 3s)}{7r} = 2r + 3s$$

Note: Since you know that to get miles per hour you divide, you can *ZAP* **F** because the items are subtracted and **G** because they are multiplied.

5-D $(2 + 3\sqrt{3})(1 - \sqrt{3})$ F.O.I.L. (First–Outer–Inner–Last)

$= 2(1) + 2(-\sqrt{3}) + 3\sqrt{3}(1) + 3\sqrt{3}(-\sqrt{3})$ Multiply the parts.

$= 2 - 2\sqrt{3} + 3\sqrt{3} - 9$ Combine like terms.

$= -7 + \sqrt{3}$

$= \sqrt{3} - 7$

6-H To change a fraction into a decimal, divide the denominator into the numerator.

F.
$$4)\overline{3.0} = .75$$
$$2\,80$$
$$\overline{20}$$
$$20$$
$$\overline{0}$$

G.
$$2)\overline{1.0} = .5$$
$$1\,0$$
$$\overline{0}$$

H.
$$9)\overline{3.0} = .33333\ldots$$
$$2\,7$$
$$\overline{30}$$
$$27$$
$$\overline{3}$$

J.
$$8)\overline{1.0} = .125$$
$$8$$
$$\overline{20}$$
$$16$$
$$\overline{40}$$
$$40$$
$$\overline{0}$$

K.
$$4)\overline{1.0} = .25$$
$$8$$
$$\overline{20}$$
$$20$$
$$\overline{0}$$

7-A If parallel lines are cut by a transversal, then corresponding angles are congruent. Since $AE \parallel BD$, $\angle CAE$ and $\angle CBD$ are corresponding angles. Therefore, $\angle CBD$ has a measure of 23°. $\angle C$ has a measure of 90° because $\triangle ACE$ is a right triangle. Since the sum of the angles in a triangle is 180°, the measure of $\angle BDC = 180° - 90° - 23° = 67°$. Together $\angle BDC$ and $\angle BDE$ make a line so the measure of $\angle BDE = 180° - 67° = 113°$.

8-H $\angle KLF$ and $\angle ELH$ are vertical angles so the measure of $\angle KLF$ is 52°. $\angle GJB$ and $\angle KLF$ are corresponding angles so the measure of $\angle GJB$ is 52° because when parallel lines are cut by a transversal, then corresponding angles are congruent.

9-C There are 360° in a circle. This arc of 8 inches is the same part of the circumference that the 40° angle is out of the 360° for the whole circle. Using c as the circumference, this can be written as a proportion.

$$\frac{40}{360} = \frac{8}{c} \qquad \text{Simplify } \frac{40}{360} \text{ to } \frac{1}{9}.$$

$$\frac{1}{9} = \frac{8}{c} \qquad \text{Cross multiply.}$$

$$c = 72$$

Since the circumference of a circle equals π times the diameter, substitute πd for c.

$$\pi d = 72 \qquad \text{Divide by } \pi.$$

$$d = \frac{72}{\pi}$$

10-H To find the average of 4 numbers, add them and divide by 4.

$$\frac{2^1 + 2^2 + 2^3 + 2^4}{4} = \frac{2 + 4 + 8 + 16}{4} = \frac{30}{4} = 7.5$$

11-C To find the average cost per item, take the total cost divided by the number of items. The cost of 15 of item A is $15x$. The cost of 10 of item B is $10y$. The cost of the A and B items together is $15x + 10y$. Since there are $15 + 10 = 25$ items, the average cost is $\frac{15x + 10y}{25}$.

12-F To factor $3x^2 - 33x + 90$, first factor out 3 to get $3(x^2 - 11x + 30)$. Finish factoring to get: $3(x - 6)(x - 5)$. Choice **F** has 2 of the factors.

13-A The area of a circle is πr^2. With the radius of $a - 3$, the area is $\pi(a - 3)^2 = \pi(a^2 - 6a + 9)$.

14-G The average of the two expressions will be their sum divided by 2.

$\frac{(3a + 7) + (4a + 1)}{2}$	Add $3a + 4a$ and $7 + 1$.
$= \frac{7a + 8}{2}$	Separate into two fractions.
$= \frac{7a}{2} + \frac{8}{2}$	Simplify $\frac{8}{2}$.
$= \frac{7a}{2} + 4$	

Note: Since the average of $3a$ and $4a$ will be between $3a$ and $4a$, the only choice with a reasonable amount of a is **G**.

15-E Look at the choices. Letter **E** has division by zero. Since division by zero is undefined, you can choose **E** even if you don't know what a rational expression is.

16-H

$-3x + 10 > 1$	The sum of -3 times x and $10 > 1$.
$-3x \geq -9$	Subtract 10.
$-3x > -9$	Divide by -3.
$x < 3$	Switch the equivalent sign.

17-C The problem tells you that $x = \frac{1}{2}y$ and that:

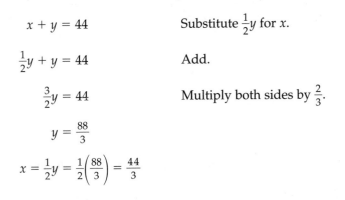

$x + y = 44$	Substitute $\frac{1}{2}y$ for x.
$\frac{1}{2}y + y = 44$	Add.
$\frac{3}{2}y = 44$	Multiply both sides by $\frac{2}{3}$.
$y = \frac{88}{3}$	
$x = \frac{1}{2}y = \frac{1}{2}\left(\frac{88}{3}\right) = \frac{44}{3}$	

The difference between x and y is $\frac{88}{3} - \frac{44}{3} = \frac{44}{3} = 14\frac{2}{3}$ miles.

18-K   Obtuse angles measure between 90° and 180°. You need to decide which of the following is TRUE:

>   **I.** Since the larger of $\angle A$ and $\angle B$ is less than 180° and the smaller one is greater than 90°, their difference must be less than 90°. TRUE.

>   **II.** Since both angles are greater than 90°, their sum is less than 180°. The sum of the three angles of a triangle is equal to 180°. FALSE.

>   **III.** Since both angles are less than 180°, their sum is less than 360°. The sum of the angles of a trapezoid is 360°, so they could be interior angles of a trapezoid. TRUE.

Note: By picking two angles slightly greater than 90° and trying to draw the 3 figures and then picking angles slightly less than 180° and trying to draw them again, you can probably decide how to *ZAP* this question.

19-C $\overline{AB} \parallel \overline{CD}$ because two lines in a plane that are both perpendicular to a third line are parallel to each other. $\angle EGH$ measures 60° because it is one angle of an equilateral triangle. $\angle AEF$ measures 60° by the theorem that states, "If two parallel lines are cut by a transversal, then alternate interior angles are congruent."

20-G   The point where any line crosses the y-axis has an x-coordinate of zero. You can find the equation of the line and substitute $x = 0$ to find the y-coordinate of the point.

The slope is $\dfrac{4-1}{1-3} = \dfrac{3}{-2} = \dfrac{-3}{2}$.

Now put the slope and the point (1, 4) into point slope form.

$$y - y_1 = m\,(x - x_1)$$

$$y - 4 = \frac{-3}{2}(x - 1) \qquad \text{Substitute } x = 0.$$

$$y - 4 = \frac{-3}{2}(0 - 1)$$

$$y - 4 = \frac{-3}{2}(-1)$$

$$y - 4 = \frac{3}{2}$$

$$y = 5\tfrac{1}{2}$$

Note: Since the point must have an x-coordinate of zero, *ZAP* **H**, **J**, and **K**. If you think of going from B to A, you go up 3 and to the left 2. Since you only need to move 1 to the left to cross the y-axis, you only need to move up $\frac{1}{2}$ of 3, or $1\frac{1}{2}$, to reach the appropriate height. Point A is already up 4 so you would end up at $4 + 1\frac{1}{2} = 5\frac{1}{2}$.

Math Answer Review
Workout E

1-D The problem gives the side opposite $\angle A$ and asks for the hypotenuse. $\text{Sin } A = \frac{\text{side opposite}}{\text{hypotenuse}}$

$$0.500 = \frac{9}{\overline{AB}} \text{ or } \overline{AB} = \frac{9}{0.500} = 18.00$$

Note: Since this is a $30°-60°-90°$ triangle, you can multiply the short leg by 2 to get the hypotenuse. $2(9) = 18$.

2-H The problem says that the total of the three days equals two thirds of his acreage:

$$\frac{2}{3}(270) = 180$$

The amount for each of the three days is 40 for Monday, x for Tuesday and $(40 + x) - 20$ or $x + 20$ for Wednesday.

$40 + x + x + 20 = 180$ Combine like terms.

$2x + 60 = 180$

3-E A diagonal divides a $90°$ angle in two. Since $\overline{BD}$ is a diagonal of the square, $\angle CBE = 45°$. This means $\triangle BEC$ is a $45°-45°-90°$ triangle. The leg $\overline{EC}$ is the hypotenuse divided by $\sqrt{2}$.

$$\frac{4}{\sqrt{2}} = \frac{4\sqrt{2}}{2} = 2\sqrt{2}$$

4-G Since the center of the circle is $(0, 0)$ and the radius is 3, the equation of the circle is:

$$(x - 0)^2 + (y - 0)^2 = 9$$

$x^2 + y^2 = 9$ Divide each side by 9.

$$\frac{x^2}{9} + \frac{y^2}{9} = 1$$

Note: For an equation to be a circle, the coefficients of the x^2 term and y^2 term must both be the same and positive when they are on the same side of the equation. You could *ZAP* **J** and **K** because they have no squared terms and **F** because the y^2 term is negative.

5-C $-(-1)^3 - (-1)^2$ Multiply the powers.

$-(-1) - (1)$ Simplify $-(-1)$.

$1 - 1$ Subtract.

0

6-F The value of any point y on the x-axis is zero.

7-B   Numbers with negative exponents are the same as the reciprocal of the number with the positive exponent. Example: $x^{\frac{-1}{2}} = \frac{1}{x^{\frac{1}{2}}}$

$$4^{\frac{-3}{2}} = \frac{1}{4^{\frac{3}{2}}} = \frac{1}{(\sqrt{4})^3} = \frac{1}{2^3} = \frac{1}{8}$$

8-J   If two sides of the right triangle are the same length, then two angles are the same and the other is 90°. That makes the triangle a 45°−45°−90° triangle. The hypotenuse is $\sqrt{2}$ times the length of a leg. $\sqrt{2}(\sqrt{5}) = \sqrt{10}$.

9-B

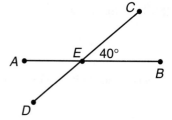

Draw a diagram to show $\overline{AB}$ intersecting $\overline{CD}$ at point E so that $\angle CEB$ looks like it measures 40°. The measure of $\angle AEC$ is 180° − 40° = 140° because together with $\angle CEB$ they form $\overline{AB}$. $\angle AEC$ and $\angle BED$ are congruent because they are vertical angles, so $\angle BED$ = 140°. The measure of $\angle AED$ is 40° because it and $\angle CEB$ are vertical angles. Obtuse angles measure more than 90°. $\angle AEC$ and $\angle BED$ are the obtuse angles.

Their sum is 140° + 140° = 280°.

Note: By looking at the diagram, you can see that there are 2 angles that are greater than 90° so they must add up to more than 180°. You can ZAP **C**, **D**, and **E**. Since the sum of all 4 angles is 360°, the sum of 2 of them must be less than 360° so you can ZAP **A**.

10-F   Since all of the equations are lines, there will not be a solution if the lines are parallel. If the lines are parallel, they have the same slope but the equations are not multiples of each other. If the equation of a line is written in the form of $y = mx + b$, then the slope is m. Write each equation in this form and see if the x coefficients are the same.

       F. $y = \frac{3}{2}x + 2$

             $y = \frac{3}{2}x + 7$

       G. $y = -3x + 4$

             $y = \frac{-3}{2}x + 4$

       H. $y = \frac{3}{2}x + \frac{11}{2}$

             $y = 3x + 7$

       J. $y = 3x + 1$

             $y = -3x + 1$

       K. $y = -\frac{1}{3}x + \frac{2}{3}$

             $y = -x + 1$

Since choice **F** is the only pair of equations with the same slope, then the lines in **F** are parallel and the system has no solution.

11-B $\overline{AB}$ is the hypotenuse of the right triangle and $\overline{CB}$ is opposite the 40° angle and adjacent to the 50° angle. To find the length of $\overline{CB}$ you would need to use sin 40° or cos 50°. By looking at the choices, you can see that only one choice uses cos 50° and none of them use sin 40°. The actual equation would be $\cos 50° = \frac{\overline{CB}}{6}$ or $\overline{CB} = 6 \cos 50°$.

12-J   Since the graph intersects the x-axis at $(-2, 0)$ and $(2, 0)$, the roots of the equation are 2 and -2. That means the equation in factored form is $y = (x - 2)(x + 2)$ or $y = x^2 - 4$. Another way to find the equation of the parabola is to use the form of a parabola $y = a(x - h)^2 + k$, where (h, k) is the vertex and a is some constant. Here the vertex is $(0, -4)$.

By substitution $y = a(x - 0)^2 + (-4)$

$$y = ax^2 - 4$$

To find a, plug in any other point on the parabola. Substituting $(2, 0)$, you get

$$0 = a(2)^2 - 4$$

$$0 = 4a - 4$$

$$4 = 4a$$

$$a = 1$$

So the equation is $y = 1x^2 - 4$ or $y = x^2 - 4$.

Note: Since the parabola opens up instead of to the side, x will be squared in the equation and not y. So you can ZAP **G** and **K**.

13-E   To see where the points are, make a coordinate axis and plot the points. Now you need to see if you can sketch each figure so that it intersects all 4 points. Each of them can be done except two perpendicular lines. Here are examples of the other 4 choices:

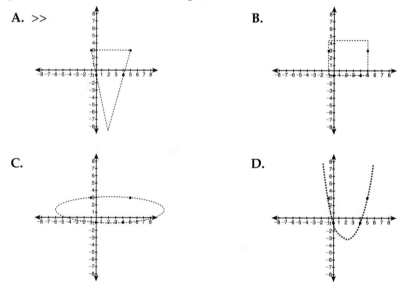

A. >>

B.

C.

D.

14-G   Since the area of the square is 64, the length of a side is $\sqrt{64} = 8$. The area of $\triangle EBD$ is

$\frac{1}{2}(\text{base} \bullet \text{height}) = \frac{1}{2}(8 \bullet 8) = 32$. The area of $\triangle ABE$ equals the area of the square minus the area

of $\triangle BCD$ and $\triangle EBD$. $64 - 20 - 32 = 12$

15-E Since the first two points are on the same horizontal line, the length of that side of the triangle is the difference of the x-coordinates. $6 - 0 = 6$. Since the last two points are on the same vertical line, the length of that side is the difference of y-coordinates $4 - 0 = 4$. Since the triangle is a right triangle, you can use the Pythagorean Theorem to find the length of the hypotenuse.

$$\sqrt{4^2 + 6^2} = \sqrt{16 + 36} = \sqrt{52}$$ The perimeter is the sum of all three sides.

$$4 + 6 + \sqrt{52} = 10 + \sqrt{52}$$

16-K $40 = (2)(20)$

$= (2)(2)(10)$

$= (2)(2)(2)(5)$

Note: To be a prime factorization, all of the factors must be prime. The first 4 answers all have factors that are not prime and can all be *ZAPPED*.

17-D Draw a coordinate axis and plot the points. The missing corner of the square is in the fourth quadrant. It has the same x-coordinate as $(1, 0)$ and the same y-coordinate as $(-2, -3)$.

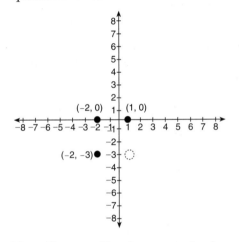

Note: If you realize that any pair of coordinates in the fourth quadrant will have a positive x-value and a negative y-value, you can *ZAP* all the other choices without figuring out the exact coordinates.

18-K $y = 2$ crosses the y-axis at $(0, 2)$. To find the distance between $(-1, -4)$ and $(0, 2)$ use the distance formula:

$$d = \sqrt{(x_2 - x_1)^2 + (y_2 - y_1)^2}$$

$$d = \sqrt{(0 - -1)^2 + (2 - -4)^2}$$

$$= \sqrt{(1)^2 + (6)^2}$$

$$= \sqrt{1 + 36}$$

$$= \sqrt{37}$$

19-D   The factors are in the form of $(a - b)(a + b)$ so their product is $a^2 - b^2$ with $a = \sqrt{39}$ and $b = 2\sqrt{7}$.

$$(\sqrt{39} - 2\sqrt{7})(\sqrt{39} + 2\sqrt{7})$$

$$= (\sqrt{39})^2 - (2\sqrt{7})^2$$

$$= 39 - (4 \bullet 7)$$

$$= 39 - 28$$

$$= 11$$

Note: You could just foil the binomials to get the answer.

20-H $6a^2 + a - 2 = 0$ Factor.

$(3a + 2)(2a - 1) = 0$ Set each factor equal to zero.

$3a + 2 = 0$ or $2a - 1 = 0$

$3a = -2$ or $2a = 1$

$a = \dfrac{-2}{3}$ or $\dfrac{1}{2}$

Since $\dfrac{1}{2}$ is larger than $\dfrac{-2}{3}$, the correct choice is $\dfrac{1}{2}$.

Math Answer Review
Workout F

1-A   Since all of the heights in the problem are between 6 feet and 7 feet, average the inches and add the average to six feet. Let x be the number of inches for the fifth player. To find the average, add the inches for the 5 players and divide by 5. The problem says the average will equal 4.

$$\frac{1 + 2 + 3 + 5 + x}{5} = 4$$ Add the numbers.

$$\frac{11 + x}{5} = 4$$ Multiply both sides of the equation by 5.

$$11 + x = 20$$ Subtract 11 from both sides.

$$x = 9$$

The player would need to be 6'9".

2-J   Since $DECB$ has 2 parallel sides, it is a trapezoid. The formula for the area of a trapezoid is:

$$A = \tfrac{1}{2}(b_1 + b_2)h$$

$$\tfrac{1}{2}(4 + 5)(2) = 9$$

3-B   The bread sells for $\frac{1}{2}$ of the regular price or $\frac{1}{2}(1.50) = 0.75$ or 75 cents. The tax is 4% of the sales price or $(.04)75 = 3$ cents. The cost, including tax, is $75 + 3 = 78$ cents.

Note: Once you figure out that the sale price is 75 cents, you know the total of the sales price and tax will be over 75 cents, so you can *ZAP* **C**, **D**, and **E**.

4-H   Use the identity $\sin^2 x + \cos^2 x = 1$.

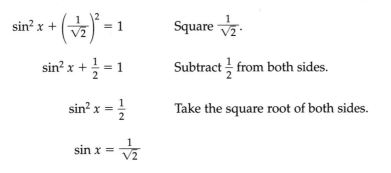

$$\sin^2 x + \left(\frac{1}{\sqrt{2}}\right)^2 = 1$$ Square $\frac{1}{\sqrt{2}}$.

$$\sin^2 x + \frac{1}{2} = 1$$ Subtract $\frac{1}{2}$ from both sides.

$$\sin^2 x = \frac{1}{2}$$ Take the square root of both sides.

$$\sin x = \frac{1}{\sqrt{2}}$$

5-B   Set up a proportion using the ratios of gallons to rooms with x as the missing amount.

$$\frac{3}{4} = \frac{\frac{1}{2}}{x}$$ Cross multiply.

$$3x = 2$$ Divide by 3.

$$x = \frac{2}{3}$$

6-G   Break 96 into its prime factors.

$$96 = 2 \bullet 48$$

$$= 2 \bullet 2 \bullet 24$$

$$= 2 \bullet 2 \bullet 2 \bullet 12$$

$$= 2 \bullet 2 \bullet 2 \bullet 2 \bullet 6$$

$$= 2 \bullet 2 \bullet 2 \bullet 2 \bullet 2 \bullet 3$$

Since 2 and 3 are the only prime factors, **G** is the correct choice.

Note: If you look at the choices, you don't need to factor 96. You can *ZAP* **F**, **H**, and **K** because they are not prime. *ZAP* **J** because 19 is not a factor of 96. 3 is a prime number and it divides into 96 without leaving a remainder so it is a factor.

7-E

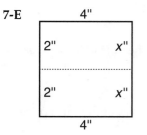

If the figure is symmetric about the dashed line, then the parts that correspond on the other side of the line are congruent. That means that the picture with all of the measurements on it looks like this. The perimeter is the distance around the figure or:

$$4 + 2 + 2 + 4 + x + x = 12 + 2x.$$

8-J

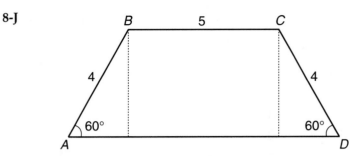

Since $ABCD$ is a trapezoid, $\overline{BC} \parallel \overline{AD}$. By the theorem that states, "If two parallel lines are cut by a transversal, then same-side interior angles are supplementary," the measure of $\angle A$ is $180° - 120° = 60°$. Since $\angle A = \angle D$, the trapezoid is isosceles and the measure of $\overline{CD}$ is 4. If you draw in the dotted lines, you get a rectangle and two $30°-60°-90°$ triangles. The short leg of each triangle is one half of the hypotenuse or $\frac{1}{2}(4) = 2$.

The length of $\overline{AD}$ is $2 + 5 + 2 = 9$.

9-C If one number is 3 and the other is x, then their product is $3x$ and their sum is $x + 3$. If their product is 5 greater than the sum, you need to add 5 to the sum to equal the product. The equation is $3x = (x + 3) + 5$.

10-K The $\csc \theta = \dfrac{1}{\sin \theta} = \dfrac{1}{\frac{5}{13}} = \dfrac{13}{5}$

11-B Because $\overline{SR} \parallel \overline{HJ}$, the measure of $\angle KSR$ is equal to the measure of $\angle KHJ$ and the measure of $\angle KRS$ is equal to the measure of $\angle KJH$ by the theorem that states, "If two parallel lines are cut by a transversal, then corresponding angles are congruent." That makes $\triangle KSR$ similar to $\triangle KHJ$ by the angle-angle similarity theorem. That means that the sides of the triangle form the proportion.

$$\frac{\overline{KR}}{\overline{KJ}} = \frac{\overline{SK}}{\overline{HK}}$$

If you let $= \overline{RJ} = x$, then the values to substitute into the proportion are:

$\overline{HK} = 6, \overline{KJ} = 4, \overline{SK} = \overline{HK} - \overline{HS} = 6 - 2 = 4$ and $\overline{KR} = \overline{KJ} - \overline{RJ} = 4 - x$.

$\dfrac{4 - x}{4} = \dfrac{4}{6}$ Cross multiply.

$6(4 - x) = 4 \bullet 4$ Simplify.

$24 - 6x = 16$ Subtract 24 from each side.

$-6x = -8$ Divide each side by -6.

$x = \dfrac{8}{6} = \dfrac{4}{3}$

12-J   The cyclist traveled 45 miles in x hours so her average speed was $\frac{45}{x}$. The problem says her average speed was $2x - 1$. So the equation to find x is

$$\frac{45}{x} = 2x - 1 \qquad\qquad \text{Multiply by } x.$$

$$45 = 2x^2 - x \qquad\qquad \text{Subtract 45.}$$

$$2x^2 - x - 45 = 0 \qquad\qquad \text{Factor.}$$

$$(2x + 9)(x - 5) = 0 \qquad\qquad \text{Set each factor} = 0.$$

$$x = \frac{-9}{2} \text{ or } x = 5$$

Since x is the number of hours, x must be 5. Her speed is $2x - 1 = 2(5) - 1 = 9$ mph, so in 2 hours she traveled $9 \cdot 2 = 18$ miles.

13-E   If a monomial has a variable, then it can only have positive integer powers of the variable. **A** has a negative power, **B** and **C** have fractional powers, and **D** is not a monomial because it is the sum of 2 monomials.

14-H $(\sqrt{5a})^2$

$$= (\sqrt{5})^2 a^2$$

$$= 5a^2$$

15-A   The equation of line l is given in slope-intercept form. ($y = mx + b$ where m is the slope). The slope of $y = \frac{1}{2}x + 3$ is $\frac{1}{2}$. Put the slope and the point $(4, 3)$ of line p into point-slope form to find the equation of line p.

$$y - 3 = \frac{1}{2}(x - 4)$$

To find where it intersects the x-axis, set $y = 0$.

$$0 - 3 = \frac{1}{2}(x - 4) \qquad\qquad \text{Multiply both sides by 2.}$$

$$-6 = x - 4 \qquad\qquad \text{Add 4 to both sides.}$$

$$-2 = x$$

16-K All of the choices in the problem are expressed in slope-intercept form, $y = mx + b$, where m is the slope and b is the y-intercept. Since the y-intercept of this graph is less than -3, the only choice that could be right is **K**. If you don't notice this, you will need to find the equation of the line. The slope of the line is the difference of the y-coordinates divided by the difference of the x-coordinates.

Be sure to subtract from the same point both times: $\dfrac{3 - (-3)}{3 - 1} = \dfrac{6}{2} = 3$

At this point, you can *ZAP* **F** and **J** because they don't have a slope of 3. Using one of the points and the slope, express the equation in point-slope form.

$y - (-3) = 3 (x - 1)$ Multiply by 3.

$y + 3 = 3x - 3$ Subtract 3 from both sides.

$y = 3x - 6$

17-C If $\overline{BC}$ is the hypotenuse, then $\angle B$ is the other acute angle, not the right angle. The sum of the measures of the angles is $180°$ so $\angle B = 180° - 90° - 35° = 55°$.

18-K To find the intersection, use linear combination. Multiply the second equation by -2 and add it to the first to get an equation with x and no y in it.

$4y + 3x = 8$ $4y + 3x = 8$

           equals

$-2(2y - 7x = 4)$ $+ -4y + 14x = -8$

                     $17x = 0$

                       $x = 0$

Now plug 0 in for x in $4y + 3x = 8$.

$4y + 3(0) = 8$

$4y = 8$

$y = 2$

The point is $(0, 2)$

Note: You can find the right point by plugging the choices into the two equations. Remember that to be correct the point must fit both equations.

19-E   The height to the base of an isosceles triangle bisects the base (cuts it into two segments of 4 each). That means that the height cuts the triangle into two right triangles with legs of 4 and 6. The hypotenuse can be found using the Pythagorean Theorem. The hypotenuse equals:

$$= \sqrt{4^2 + 6^2}$$

$$= \sqrt{16 + 36}$$

$$= \sqrt{52}$$

$$= \sqrt{4 \cdot 13}$$

$$= 2\sqrt{13}$$

The perimeter of the isosceles triangle is $2\sqrt{13} + 2\sqrt{13} + 8 = 8 + 4\sqrt{13}$.

20-K   The cot A is the ratio of the side adjacent to A, which is 5, to the side opposite A, which is 7. The

cot $A = \frac{5}{7}$.

Math Answer Review
Workout G

1-B To find the city's population, take 10% of 100,000 and add it to 100,000.

$$100,000 \times .1 = 10,000$$

$$100,000 + 10,000 = 110,000$$

Since 10% of the population supports Jones, take $\frac{1}{10}$ of $110,000 = \frac{110,000}{10}$.

2-F Since the axis of the parabola is vertical, you can *ZAP* **H**, **J**, and **K** because the *x* should be squared, not the *y*. By just plugging in one of the points, you can decide whether **F** or **G** is the correct choice. (0, 0) works in both equations, but any of the other points only works in equation **F**.

3-B $6b$ less than a is $a - 6b$.

$7b$ less than a is $a - 7b$.

Take the product of these two expressions.

$(a - 6b)(a - 7b)$ Multiply.

$= a^2 - 7ab - 6ab + 42b^2$ Combine the middle terms.

$= a^2 - 13ab + 42b^2$

4-H For a quadratic equation to have two real roots that are equal, the discriminant, $b^2 - 4ac$ must be equal to zero. Find the discriminant for each of the choices.

    F. $3^2 - 4(0)(2) = 9 - 0 = 9$

    G. $2^2 - 4(3)(1) = 4 - 12 = -9$

    H. $2^2 - 4(1)(1) = 4 - 4 = 0$

    J. $0^2 - 4(1)(1) = 0 - 4 = -4$

    K. $1^2 - 4(0)(0) = 1 - 0 = 1$

Note: If you didn't know about the discriminant, you could find the solutions by using the whole quadratic formula and see which choice will produce a solution with two equal real roots.

5-B $\frac{17}{50}$ means 17 divided by 50.

$$
\begin{array}{r}
.34 \\
50\overline{)17.0} \\
15.0 \\
\hline
2\,00 \\
2\,00 \\
\hline
0
\end{array}
$$

Note: Since the denominator is 50, you could multiply the numerator and denominator by 2 to get a denominator of 100 and a numerator of 34. $\frac{34}{100}$ is 34 hundredths or .34. Also, notice that $\frac{17}{50}$ is less than 1 so you can *ZAP* **E.** $\frac{17}{50}$ is greater than $\frac{17}{100}$ so you can *ZAP* **A.**

6-K   Put the points into the distance formula.

$$d = \sqrt{(x_1 - x_2)^2 + (y_1 - y_2)^2}$$

$$= \sqrt{(-4 - 2)^2 + (3 + 5)^2}$$

$$= \sqrt{(-6)^2 + (-2)^2}$$

$$= \sqrt{(36 + 4)}$$

$$= \sqrt{40}$$

$$= \sqrt{4 \cdot 10}$$

$$= 2\sqrt{10}$$

7-B   To find the solution to a quadratic equation, first get zero on one side of the equation.

$$8y^2 - 12y = -4$$ Add 4 to each side.

$$8y^2 - 12y + 4 = 0$$ Divide by 4.

$$2y^2 - 3y + 1 = 0$$ Factor.

$$(2y - 1)(y - 1) = 0$$ Set each factor equal to zero.

$$2y - 1 = 0 \text{ or } y - 1 = 0$$ Solve for y.

$$2y = 1 \quad y = 1$$

$$y = \frac{1}{2}$$

$$y = \left(\frac{1}{2}, 1\right)$$

$\frac{1}{2}$ is the smaller of the two solutions.

Note: You could find the correct choice to this problem by starting with the smallest choice given and substituting it for y in the equation. If it doesn't work, then try the next smallest and keep going until you find one that works.

8-F   The question says that $\angle B$ of the triangle is obtuse. That means that the measure of $\angle B$ is greater than $90°$. Since the sum of all three angles of a triangle is $180°$, the total of $\angle A$ and $\angle C$ must be less than $90°$ so each of them must be less than $90°$.

9-D   The line with equation $x = -3$ is a vertical line where every point on the line has an x-value of -3. The shortest distance from a point to a line is the segment that is perpendicular to the line that ends in the point. In this case, that is the part of the x-axis from $(-3, 0)$ to $(0, 0)$. The distance between them is 3.

Note: It might help to draw a diagram with a coordinate system showing the point and the line.

10-K   To solve a quadratic equation, get zero on one side of the equation by itself.

$$4x - x^2 = 3$$ Subtract 3 from each side.

$$4x - x^2 - 3 = 0$$ Multiply by -1 to get the x^2 term to be positive.

$$-4x + x^2 + 3 = 0$$ Rearrange the terms in order.

$$x^2 - 4x + 3 = 0$$ Factor.

$$(x - 3)(x - 1) = 0$$ Set each factor equal to 0.

$$x - 3 = 0 \text{ or } x - 1 = 0$$

$$x = 3 \text{ or } x = 1$$

Note: You can find the right choice by plugging in some of the answers for x. ZAP all answers that don't work.

11-E   "3 more than four times y" is the expression $4y + 3$.

"4 more than 2 times y" is the expression $2y + 4$.

Their product is:

$(4y + 3)(2y + 4)$ Foil.

$= 4y(2y) + 4y(4) + 3(2y) + 3(4)$ Multiply the constants.

$= 8y^2 + 16y + 6y + 12$ Add the middle terms.

$= 8y^2 + 22y + 12$

12-J   To simplify the product, use the foil method.

$(1 + \sqrt{7})(3 + \sqrt{7})$

$= 3 + \sqrt{7} + 3\sqrt{7} + 7$ Add the 3 and 7 and $\sqrt{7}$ to $3\sqrt{7}$.

$= 10 + 4\sqrt{7}$

13-E   Since $a = b$, substitute b for a in each equation and simplify to see if the sides of the equation are the same.

A. $\dfrac{xa}{xb} = 1$ **B.** $x^a + x^b = 2x^a$ **C.** $x^{a+b} = x^{2a}$

$\dfrac{xa}{xa} = 1$ $x^a + x^a = 2x^a$ $x^{a+a} = x^{2a}$

$1 = 1$ $2x^a = 2x^a$ $x^{2a} = x^{2a}$

TRUE   **TRUE**   **TRUE**

D. $x^{a-2b} = \dfrac{1}{x^a}$ **E.** $(x^a)(x^b) = x^{ab}$

$x^{a-2a} = \dfrac{1}{x^a}$ $(x^a)(x^a) = x^{a \bullet a}$

$x - a = \dfrac{1}{x^a}$ $x^{a+a} = xa^2$

$\dfrac{1}{x^a} = \dfrac{1}{x^a}$ $x^{2a} = xa^2$

TRUE   **TRUE**

Remember that when you multiply powers of the same base, you add the exponents.

14-F To find the possible values of x, solve the inequality.

$3 - 13x > 19$ Subtract 3 from each side.

$-13x > 16$ Divide by -13.

$x < \frac{-16}{3}$ Reverse the inequality sign.

The only choice that is less than $\frac{-16}{3}$ is -2.

Note: You can find the correct choice by plugging the values in for x in $3 - 13x$ and finding out if the value you get is greater than 19.

15-C To factor $8r^4s^3 - 4r^3s^2$, factor out the largest constant and the largest power of each variable that is in both terms. $4r^3s^2$ is the greatest common factor. The remaining factor is $(2rs - 1)$. Compare each of the choices to $4r^3s^2$. The correct answer can't have a constant that isn't a factor of 4, a power of r greater than 3, or a power of s greater than 2. The only choice that works is $4r^3$.

Note: You could look at the choices and see which one is a factor of the polynomial by checking to see if it is a factor of each of the two monomial terms. All of the choices are factors of $8r^4s^3$ so check each choice to see if it is a factor of $4r^3s^2$. Since 8 is not a factor, ZAP **A** and **D**. Since r^4 is not a factor, ZAP **B** and **E**.

16-H To find the slope of a line, take the difference of the y-coordinates divided by the difference of the x-coordinates $\frac{y - y_1}{x - x_1}$.

$$\frac{2 - 1}{4 - (-1)} = \frac{1}{4 + 1} = \frac{1}{5}$$

Note: A slope that goes up and to the right is positive so ZAP **F** and **G**.

17-C If $ABCD$ is a rectangle, then $\angle A$ is a right angle. From $\angle ADB$ the problem gives the side adjacent as 4 and you want to know the hypotenuse. Cos $x = \frac{\text{adjacent}}{\text{hypotenuse}}$

$\cos 47° = \frac{4}{x}$ Multiply by x.

$x \cos 47° = 4$ Divide by $\cos 47°$.

$x = \frac{4}{\cos 47}$ Substitute $\frac{1}{\sec} 47°$ for $\cos 47°$.

$\frac{4}{\frac{1}{\sec 47°}}$

$x = 4 \sec 47°$

Note: You can ZAP **A** because with a 47° angle, the answer is not going to be an integer. You can ZAP **E** because cot uses the two legs of the right triangle, not the hypotenuse.

18-F   In Quadrant III, both of the coordinates are negative.

19-D   In an equilateral triangle, all sides are the same length. To make this problem easier, you could draw two equilateral triangles and label their vertices. Make sure that the triangles are not the same size. Now look at each proportion and see if it is true.

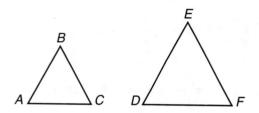

    I. Since sides *AB* and *BC* are the same length, both ratios are equal to 1 and the proportion is TRUE.

    II. Statement II says that the ratio of one side of the first triangle to one side of the second is the same as the ratio of one side of the second triangle to one side of the first. This would only be true if the triangles were the same size. Statement II is FALSE.

    III. Both ratios in this proportion compare one side of the first triangle to a side of the second triangle. Since all sides of each triangle are the same, this proportion is TRUE.

20-H   By breaking 1000 into its factors, you can find the prime factorization.

$$1000 = 10 \times 100$$
$$= 10 \times 10 \times 10$$
$$= 2 \times 5 \times 2 \times 5 \times 2 \times 5$$

Since 2 and 5 are the only prime factors, **H** is the correct choice.

Note: If you look at the choices, you can find the correct one without finding the prime factorization. *ZAP* **G**, **J**, and **K** because they are not prime numbers. *ZAP* **F** because 3 is not a factor of 1000. That leaves 5. 5, which is a prime number and it divides into 1000 without leaving a remainder so it is a factor.

Math Answer Review
Workout H

1-A   To get the product, use the F.O.I.L. method and multiply each of the two parts of the first factor times each of the two parts of the second factor. Remember to keep the negative sign with its term.

$$(a^x + b^y)(2a^x - b^y)$$

$$= a^x(2a^x) + a^x(-b^y) + b^y(2a^x) + b^y(-b^y)$$

You can simplify the first and last terms. Since they each have the same base, just add the exponents.

$$= 2a^{2x} + a^x(-b^y) + b^y(2a^x) - b^{2y}$$

Now rearrange and combine the two middle terms.

$$= 2a^{2x} - a^x b^y + 2a^x b^y - b^{2y}$$

$$= 2a^{2x} + a^x b^y - b^{2y}$$

2-H   You can tell by looking at the problem that the value will always be greater than 1 because $x + 1$ is always greater than $x - 1$ for all $x > 2$. You can *ZAP* **J** and **K**. Since the expression must be true for all $x > 2$, plug in any number greater than 2. Set $x = 3$.

$$\frac{3 + 1}{3 - 1} = \frac{4}{2} = 2$$

Since this contradicts both **F** and **G**, you can *ZAP* them. **H** is the only answer left.

3-D   Set up an equation. To find the value of x, you need to start at the end of the sentence and work backwards. "The number obtained by subtracting 210 from x" is $x - 210$. "The number which is 6 times that number" is $6(x - 210)$. The number that is "ten greater than" that number is $6(x - 210) + 10$.

$x = 6(x - 210) + 10$	Simplify.
$x = 6x - 1260 + 10$	Add the 2 numbers.
$x = 6x - 1250$	Subtract $6x$.
$-5x = -1250$	Divide by -5.
$x = 250$	

4-J   To solve this, write the number of pencils that each person has in terms of x. If $x = $ the number of pencils that Ann owns, then $2x = $ the number of pencils that Mary owns and $2x + 10 = $ the number of pencils that Bill and Frank own together. If you add all of the pencils together you will get 85. That means that $x + 2x + 2x + 10 = 85$. Adding the x terms together you get $5x + 10 = 85$.

Note: Since Mary owns $2x$, the total for all four can't be less than $2x$, so you can *ZAP* **F**. Since Mary and Ann together own $3x$, you can *ZAP* **H** for the same reason.

5-C To find the area of the figure, draw in a line to break the figure into a rectangle and a triangle.

The area of the rectangle is the base times the height or $7 \cdot 2 = 14$. The area of the triangle is one

half times the base times the height. The base of the triangle is $9 - 7$ or 2 and the height is $2 - x$.

The area of the triangle is $\frac{1}{2} \cdot 2 \cdot (2 - x) = 2 - x$. The total area of the figure is

$14 + 2 - x$ or $16 - x$.

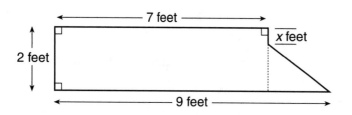

6-K A question with choices like these is really the same as three true-false questions. In making the correct choice, you need to look at each statement together with the information in the question and decide, "Is this true all of the time?" If you know a theorem that says it is not, or can draw a picture to show that in at least one case it is not true, then you know the statement is not a correct choice.

    I. Here is a picture that shows statement I is false.

        <<graphic>>

    II. Statement II is true because it is the contrapositive of the theorem that states "if parallel lines are cut by a transversal, then alternate interior angles are congruent." The contrapositive would read, "If a transversal to two lines forms alternate interior angles that are not congruent, then the lines are not parallel."

    III. If angles F and G were equal, then $\overline{AD}$ would be equal to $\overline{BC}$. However, since $\angle F$ is smaller than $\angle G$, it means that $\overline{AB}$ is tipped downward on the A end toward $\overline{DC}$. Therefore, $\overline{AD}$ must be shorter than $\overline{BC}$.

Since statements II and III are true, the answer is **K**.

7-C If a number is a factor of 124, then it divides evenly into 124 and leaves a remainder of zero. To find the choice that doesn't work, divide each number into 124.

    A. $\begin{array}{r} 62 \\ 2\overline{)124} \\ 12 \\ \hline 04 \\ 4 \\ \hline 0 \end{array}$ **B.** $\begin{array}{r} 31 \\ 4\overline{)124} \\ 12 \\ \hline 04 \\ 4 \\ \hline 0 \end{array}$ **C.** $\begin{array}{r} 15 \\ 8\overline{)124} \\ 8 \\ \hline 44 \\ 40 \\ \hline 4 \end{array}$

Note: When you divide 2 into 124 you get 62, so you know 62 is a factor and you can *ZAP* **A** and **E**. When you divide 4 into 124, you get 31 so you can *ZAP* **B** and **D**. That only leaves **C**.

8-G One easy way to solve this problem is to draw a line connecting B and F. Now you see 8 triangles, each with an area of 12.5 square units. To get the area of $HBCD$, simply multiply 12.5 times 3.

9-A Start with the equation for the circumference of a circle $C = 2\pi r$. Substitute $4a + 3b$ for r and

$\dfrac{8a^2 + 6ab}{2}$ for C. Then solve for π.

$$C = 2\pi r$$

$\dfrac{8a^2 + 6ab}{2} = 2\pi(4a + 3b)$ Divide by 2 and $(4a + 3b)$.

$\dfrac{8a^2 + 6ab}{2 \bullet 2\,(4a + 3b)} = \pi$ Leave the denominator in factored form and factor the numerator.

$\dfrac{2a(4a + 3b)}{2 \bullet 2(4a + 3b)} = \pi$ Cancel one 2 and $(4a + 3b)$.

$\dfrac{a}{2} = \pi$

10-F To simplify the expression, first remember to subtract each of the terms in the second part.

$x^2y + 2y^2 - 3x^2 - (-4x^2 + 3y^2 - 2x^2y)$

$= x^2y + 2y^2 - 3x^2 + 4x^2 - 3y^2 + 2x^2y$ Combine the similar terms.

$= 3x^2y - y^2 + x^2$ Rearrange the terms to match choice **F**.

Note: Since nothing is multiplied, you can't get any terms with powers that are greater than 2, so you can ZAP **J** and **K**.

11-B Simplify each expression and then take the absolute value.

A. $|(-1)(-1)| = |1| = 1$

B. $|(1 - 8)| = |-7| = 7$

C. $|(-1)(0)| = |0| = 0$

D. $|(-2)(-1)| = |2| = 2$

E. $\left|-\dfrac{1}{8}\right| = \dfrac{1}{8}$

12-K The area of the circle is πr^2 where r is the radius of the circle. The radius of a circle is one half the diameter. The radius of circle A is 3 so the area of circle A is $9\pi^2$. The radius of circle B is $\dfrac{x}{2}$ so the area of circle B is $\dfrac{x^2\pi}{4}$. The ratio of A's area to B's area is $\dfrac{9\pi}{x^2\pi} = \dfrac{36}{x^2}$ or $36{:}x^2$.

Note: If you know the ratio of any two corresponding linear measures of two similar figures, then the ratio of the areas is the original ratio squared. All circles are similar to each other so here the ratio of the diameters is $6{:}x$ and the ratio of the areas is $36{:}x^2$.

13-D   To find the slope of a line when you are given two points on the line, take the difference of the y-coordinates and divide by the difference of the x-coordinates. Be sure to subtract from the coordinates of the same point both times. If you subtract $(-3, -1)$ from the point $(0, 5)$ you get

$$\frac{5 - (-1)}{0 - (-3)} = \frac{5 + 1}{3} = \frac{6}{3} = 2$$

14-F   The tangent of an angle is the ratio of the side opposite that angle to the side adjacent to that angle. Since the problem doesn't give or ask for the hypotenuse, you can't use the sin or cos to solve it so you can *ZAP* **D** and look at the two ways to use the tangent.

$$\tan 55° = \frac{11}{\overline{CB}} \text{ or } \tan 35 = \frac{\overline{CB}}{11}$$

$$\overline{CB} = \frac{11}{\tan} 55° \text{ or } \overline{CB} = 11 \tan 35°$$

15-C   No special information is given about the triangle. The sum of the measures of the angles of a triangle is $180°$. $x° + y° + z° = 180$.

Subtract $z°$ from both sides $x° + y° = (180 - z)°$.

16-F   Sides AB and BC are both 5 and the perimeter is 18 so side AC is $18 - 5 - 5 = 8$ units long. Because AB and BC are the same, the altitude to side AC must divide it into two equal segments so AD is 4 units long. By the Pythagorean Theorem

$$(BD)^2 + (AD)^2 = (AB)^2$$

$$(BD)^2 + (4)^2 = 5^2$$

$$(BD)^2 = 25 - 16$$

$$BD = \sqrt{9} = 3$$

$$BD = 3$$

The area of a triangle is one half of the base times the height. Here the base is 8 and the height is

3 so the area is $\frac{1}{2}(4)(3) = 6$.

17-D   If A and B are both on a line parallel to the x-axis then they have the same y-coordinate. Since the y-coordinate of point A is 3, the y-coordinate of point B must be 3. To be in Quadrant II, point B must have a negative y-coordinate. The only choice that meets both requirements is $(-1, 3)$.

Note: You could just draw a line on the diagram that goes through A and is parallel to the x-axis. Then find each of the points listed in the choices and see which one is on the line and in Quadrant II.

18-J   Since $\triangle ABD$ is equilateral, $\angle B$ is 60° and $\triangle ABC$ is a 30°−60°−90° triangle. Since $\overline{AC}$ is 6, $\overline{BC}$ is

$\frac{6}{\sqrt{3}}$ units and $\overline{AB}$ is $2\left(\frac{6}{\sqrt{3}}\right)$ units.

The perimeter of $\triangle ABC$ is $6 + \frac{6}{\sqrt{3}} + 2\left(\frac{6}{\sqrt{3}}\right)$.

$$= 6 + \frac{6}{\sqrt{3}} + \frac{12}{\sqrt{3}}$$

$$= 6 + \frac{18}{\sqrt{3}} \qquad\qquad \text{Find a common denominator.}$$

$$= \frac{6\sqrt{3} + 18}{\sqrt{3}} \qquad\qquad \text{Multiply by } \frac{\sqrt{3}}{\sqrt{3}} \text{ to rationalize the denominator.}$$

$$= \frac{18 + 18\sqrt{3}}{3} \qquad\qquad \text{Divide both parts of the numerator by 3.}$$

$$= 6 + 6\sqrt{3}$$

19-E   If a monomial has a variable, the variable can only have positive integer exponents. You can *ZAP*

A and **B** because $\frac{3}{4}$ has no variable. *ZAP* **C** because $\sqrt{3x} = (3x)\frac{1}{2}$. *ZAP* **D** because

$\frac{3}{x} = 3(x^{-1})$.

20-K   The center of the square has coordinates (2, 2) so $\frac{e}{f} = \frac{2}{2} = 1$.

Math Answer Review
Workout I

1-E   The inequality $x - 2 \geq x - 4$ means that when you subtract 2 from x, your answer is greater than or equal to the number you get when you subtract 4 from x. That is true for all real numbers so the correct graph is **K**. If you try to solve the inequality, notice what happens.

$x - 2 \geq x - 4$ Add 2 to both sides.

$x \geq x - 2$ Subtract x from both sides.

$0 \geq -2$

Since this statement is always true, all real numbers will work for x.

2-K   Negative exponents are the same as the reciprocal of the same base with the positive of the exponent.

$$3(3^{-3}) + 9(3^{-1})$$

$$= 3\left(\frac{1}{3^3}\right) + 9\left(\frac{1}{3}\right)$$

$$= 3\left(\frac{1}{27}\right) + \frac{9}{3}$$

$$= \frac{3}{27} + 3$$

$$= \frac{1}{9} + 3$$

$$= 3\frac{1}{9}$$

3-B   Let x = the cost of the fourth car. To find the average cost of the 4 cars, add all 4 prices and divide by 4. The problem says the average is $10,000.

$\frac{8,400 + 8,400 + 8,400 + x}{4} = 10,000$ Add the cost of the first 3 cars.

$\frac{25,200 + x}{4} = 10,000$ Multiply both sides of the equation by 4.

$25,200 + x = 40,000$ Subtract 25,200 from both sides.

$x = \$14,800$

Note: You could work this problem by trying the different choices to see which one works.

4-F $\angle AGH$ has the same measure as $\angle DHF$ because when parallel lines are cut by a transversal, then corresponding angles are congruent. Since $\angle AGH$ measures 145°, $\angle BGF$ measures $180° - 145° = 35°$ because together they make a line.

5-E   If the equation of a line is in standard form $Ax + By = C$, then the slope is $\frac{-A}{B}$. In this case that is

$\frac{-4}{-1} = 4$. If you didn't know that, you could change the line into the

slope-intercept form:

$y = mx + b$ where m is the slope.

$4x - y = 3$	Subtract $4x$ from both sides.
$-y = -4x + 3$	Multiply both sides by -1.
$y = 4x - 3$	

In this form, the x-coefficient is the slope.

6-J   Finding the number halfway between two numbers is the same as finding their average. Add the two numbers together and divide by 2.

$$\frac{\frac{7}{8} + 1\frac{1}{16}}{2}$$ Change $\frac{7}{8}$ to $\frac{14}{16}$ and $1\frac{1}{16}$ to $\frac{17}{16}$.

$$= \frac{\frac{14}{16} + \frac{17}{16}}{2}$$ Add the numerators to add the fractions.

$$= \frac{\frac{31}{16}}{2}$$ Dividing by 2 is the same as multiplying by $\frac{1}{2}$.

$$= \frac{31}{32}$$

Note: Since $\frac{7}{8}$ is a little less than 1, and $1\frac{1}{16}$ is a little more than 1, the number halfway between must be very close to 1. You can ZAP **G** and **K** because they are not close to 1. Since $1\frac{1}{16} = \frac{17}{16}$, you can also ZAP **H**.

7-E   The words in the problem translate into the inequality $-4x > 3x - 17$.

$-4x > 3x - 17$	Subtract $3x$ from both sides.
$-7x > -17$	Divide both sides by -7.
$x < \frac{17}{7}$	Change the inequality sign.

8-K The equation for the area of a circle is

$A = \pi r^2$ Substitute $2a - 3b$ for r.

$A = \pi(2a - 3b)^2$ Square $2a - 3b$.

$A = \pi(4a^2 - 12ab + 9b^2)$ Multiply each term by π.

$A = 4a^2\pi - 12ab\pi + 9b^2\pi$

Note: As soon as you realize that the Area $= \pi(2a - 3b)^2$, you can see that the correct answer is π times some squared terms of a and b and you can ZAP every choice except **K**.

9-E The speeds for each of the first three hours are 360, 540, and 540. Their average is:

$$\frac{360 + 540 + 540}{3} = \frac{1440}{3} = 480$$

10-H The measure of the angle inside the triangle next to $\angle A$ is $180° - 115° = 65°$ because together they form a line. The measure of the angle next to $\angle B$ is $180° - 140° = 40°$ for the same reason. The angle inside the triangle at the same vertex as $\angle C$ has the same measure as $\angle C$ because they are vertical angles. Since the sum of all angles in a triangle must $= 180°$, the angle inside the triangle $= 180° - 65° - 40° = 75°$.

$\angle C = 75°$

11-D The perimeter of the triangle equals the sum of the 3 sides. The problem says that the perimeter is 16 so $2x^2 + 7x + 1 = 16$. Solve the equation for x.

$2x^2 + 7x + 1 = 16$

$2x^2 + 7x - 15 = 0$

$(2x - 3)(x + 5) = 0$

$2x - 3 = 0$ or $x + 5 = 0$

$x = \frac{3}{2}$ or $x = -5$

x can't be -5 because $7x$ would be -35 and the length of the side of a triangle can't be negative. x must be $\frac{3}{2}$.

$$2x^2 = 2\left(\frac{3}{2}\right)^2 = 2\left(\frac{9}{4}\right) = \frac{9}{2} \text{ or } 4.5$$

$$7x = 7\left(\frac{3}{2}\right) = \frac{21}{2} \text{ or } 10.5.$$

Since the third side is 1, the longest side is 10.5.

12-J If a segment fits inside a triangle, then the length of the segment must be less than the longest side of the triangle. The longest side of this triangle is 5.

13-D   Let x = the number of cars sold in January. He sold 4 more in February than January so he sold x + 4 in February. He sold half as many in January as he did in March so he sold twice as many in March as he did in January. That means he sold $2x$ cars in March. The total of the three months is $x + x + 4 + 2x$ or $4x + 4$. He sold 40 total so $4x + 4 = 40$. Subtract 4 from each side: $4x = 36$. Divide by 4: $x = 9$.

14-J $\angle BCA$ and $\angle BCD$ form a line together so $\angle BCA = 180° - 135° = 45°$. That makes $\triangle ABC$ a $45°-45°-90°$ triangle. $\overline{AC}$ is the hypotenuse so it has a measure of $x\sqrt{2}$.

15-B   Let x = the number of cars that Garage A will hold. Garage B holds 200 cars less than Garage A, or $x - 200$ cars. Since Garage C holds 150 cars more than Garage A, or $x + 150$ cars. Together they hold 1300 cars.

$$x + x - 200 + x + 150 = 1300$$

$$3x - 50 = 1300$$

$$3x = 1350$$

$$x = 450 \text{ cars}$$

16-G   A line that is parallel to mn must have the same slope as mn. The slope is the difference of the y-coordinates divided by the difference of the x-coordinates. Be sure to subtract from the coordinates of the same point both times.

$$\frac{6-2}{3-1} = \frac{4}{2} = 2$$

Choice **J** is not a line because of the x^2 term and can be *ZAPPED* right away. The other choices are all in slope-intercept form so the slope is the coefficient of the x term. $y = 2x - 4$ has an x coefficient of 2 so **G** is the right choice.

17-B   If you don't know that the product of a rational and an irrational number is irrational, then you can still *ZAP* **A** and **C** because being positive or negative doesn't have anything to do with being rational or irrational. To find the correct choice, pick a rational number like 4 and an irrational number like $\sqrt{2}$. When you multiply, you get $4\sqrt{2}$, which is irrational.

18-K x apples at 15 cents each would cost $15x$. y pears at 10 cents each would cost $10y$. The cost of both together is $15x + 10y$. The sales tax is 5% of the cost or $(.05)(15x + 10y)$. To find the total cost, the sales tax is added to the cost to get $(15x + 10y) + (15x + 10y)(.05)$.

19-C   The csc A is the ratio of the hypotenuse to the side opposite A. In this problem that is $\frac{5}{4}$.

20-H   Plug in each value of x in each equation and see what you get with each choice.

     F. $3(3) - 1 = 9 - 1 = 8$ $3(5) - 1 = 15 - 1 = 14$

     G. $2(3) + 2 = 6 + 2 = 8$ $2(5) + 2 = 10 + 2 = 12$

     H. $(3)^2 - 1 = 9 - 1 = 8$ $(5)^2 - 1 = 25 - 1 = 24$

     J. $(3)^2 + 1 = 9 + 1 = 10$ $(5)^2 + 1 = 25 + 1 = 26$

     K. $5(3) - 1 = 15 - 1 = 14$ $5(5) - 1 = 25 - 1 = 24$

H is the correct choice because you get 8 when you plug in 3 and 24 when you plug in 5.

Reading Answer Review
Workout A

1-A   A main idea is supported throughout a passage and not just in a few paragraphs. The passage builds to a point that is stated in the last paragraph—that the Earth has a potent and vastly underrated capacity to keep itself healthy. The rest of the choices are too specific.

2-G   Lines 57–58 say "three and a half billion years ago, at the dawn of organic evolution . . ."

3-D   From lines 40–43, you can deduce that burning fossil fuels is a cause of increased levels of carbon dioxide. Before humans began burning fossil fuels, the concentration of carbon dioxide was two hundredths of a percent; now, after thousands of years of burning fossil fuels, the concentration is three hundredths of a percent.

4-G   The point of the paragraph is that no matter how substantial the abuse to this planet, Earth has the capacity to regenerate itself. A description of "moderate" toxic dumping does nothing to strengthen this argument. So you can ZAP **F**. The same is true of **H** and **J**. A description of a dumping that was "undeniably" toxic, however, would make sense in this context.

5-D   This question has a negative twist, asking which activity would Gaia NOT be responsible for. Answers **A**, **B**, and **C** are supported by the passage. See lines 50–52 (**A**), 53–54 (**B**), and 23 (**C**).

6-J   Lines 76–79 say that a nuclear war of major proportions would affect the participants but would not disturb Gaia. In other words, a nuclear war would destroy many forms of life, but it would not destroy the planet.

7-C   Lines 67–69 say that Gaia provides oxygen by splitting CO_2 during photosynthesis.

8-G   Line 2 refers to Gaia as "the largest of all living creatures." "Creature" implies a comparison to an animal rather than a computer, a formula, or a reaction.

9-D   According to the passage, Gaia is responsible for the salinity of the oceans, the quantity of CO_2 in the atmosphere, and the existence of life; but notice that **A**, **B**, and **C** are not accurate statements according to the passage. Only **D** accurately states an effect of Gaia. Lines 53–70 describe how Gaia is responsible for the environment which provides oxygen and the forms of life which use it.

10-F   Lines 16–18 mention that life created its physical environment.

11-C   Although Hannah is looking at a field which shows both the results of the recent harvest and the effects of the wheat trucks, she is not thinking about these things (**A** and **D**). Instead, she is thinking about the ranch when Selma moved there. (**C**): "*She wondered* what it must have been like when Selma . . ." The narrator also describes some of Hannah's childhood memories, but there is no indication that these memories are part of her current thoughts. In fact, we are specifically told that she is unable to remember the last time she had walked there. In the fiction passages on the ACT Reading Test, it is often necessary to recognize the narrator's voice and to understand what information comes from the narrator and what information comes from the narrator's knowledge of the characters' thoughts.

12-G   In paragraph 3 we are told that Hannah walked a little more than a mile to the top of a hill from which she could see the canyon nearby. The passage tells us that the ranch is half a day's ride from Alderdale (lines 14–15), so **F** can be ZAPPED. The river lies well beyond the canyon (line 29) so **H** can be ZAPPED. The bluffs (**J**) are next to the hill Hannah is standing on, so they can't be a half day's ride from the ranch. **J** can be ZAPPED.

13-C   In lines 48–49, we are told "This *wind* welcomed her, like she belonged here."

14-G   The verb "slink" suggests creeping or crawling close to the ground. The narrator describes the canyon as "slinking through the hills." This figurative language creates an image of the canyon curving around the bases of a number of hills as it approaches the river, taking an indirect path because the hills are in the way. "Winding" (**G**) is the choice which best describes this. None of the other choices are suggested by the image.

15-B   The question is difficult because you must understand the whole passage to understand Hannah's mood. A nostalgic tone is hinted at throughout the passage. In lines 15–18, she reminisces about imagining the ranch house and yard as a ship. Paragraph 5 is primarily about her reminiscence of the land in general. In lines 37–40, she reminisces about being afraid of animals when she was younger, but the words, "She smiled" suggest that she is not afraid now—ZAP **C**. Nothing in the passage suggests that she is angry (**A**). Coot only comes along in the last two paragraphs; most of her walk was without him—ZAP **D**.

16-F   Lines 41–49 mention the effect of the wind on Hannah. Not only does the wind remind Hannah of the feeling of being in the airplane, it also "grab[s] her by the shoulders, shake[s] her . . ." This is a strong effect. **G** cannot be correct, for line 48 says the wind "welcomed Hannah" not frightened her. **H** is incorrect because a comparison of the wind to an airplane has nothing to do with the old woman cited in line 51. **J** implies that Hannah's imagination is not to be trusted and that she "wildly exaggerates things." The tone of the passage suggests that although Hannah has a vivid imagination, she still has her senses about her.

17-A   This question tests your ability to carefully read and interpret lines 50–54. The first sentence is a bit backwards: "She had learned to recognize *her* voice in these . . . winds"—who does *her* refer to? The next line tells you: "the voice of the old woman she imagined as the land" who, according to lines 53–54 is, "a combination of all the generations who had lived or wandered here." **B** is wrong because Selma is a real person (see line 12), not a voice in the wind. **C** is wrong because Hannah's family is not mentioned in relation to the wind. And **D** is wrong because "an old woman who once owned the land" suggests a real person, not an imaginary voice in the wind.

18-H   As you read the passage, you need to understand what Hannah is doing and why she is doing it. Hannah behaves as someone would who has grown up there and has been away for several years. Lines 15–16 give the best clue: "When Hannah was growing up . . ." and goes on to mention how she imagined the ranch back then. Again in lines 37–38 we get a clue that Hannah grew up on the ranch: "She smiled, remembering when she used to be afraid of the coyotes and bobcats." And we know that although Hannah has been away, she refers to the ranch house as home (line 70). **F** is wrong because no mention is made of Hannah's staying with Selma. **G** is wrong because the passage never says that Hannah has moved back to the ranch. **J** is wrong because the passage doesn't mention that she spent only her summers at the ranch.

19-B   This question asks you to picture a simile. Hannah imagined that the ranch house and its yard was a ship "floating through the brown-yellow wheat field" (lines 17–18). If the house is a ship, then the field is water. **A** is NOT correct because Hannah included the green grass surrounding the house as part of the ship (line 16).

20-J   This question has a negative twist because it asks which statement is NOT supported. Although Hannah decides to return to the ranch (in the last paragraph), nothing says she really wants to be with the people there, so **J** is NOT supported. Answer **F** is supported in lines 25–26: "Whenever she remembered the ranch, this [the canyon] was the place she thought of." **G** is supported. The tone of the whole passage suggests that Hannah feels close to the land; we don't know if she feels that close to the people. And Coot, the dog, did startle her (**H**).

Reading Answer Review
Workout B

1-A   Lines 17–18 contain the topic sentence of the paragraph, which says "the acquisition of language by children may offer insights into the origins of speech." Choices **B** and **D** are very *ZAPPABLE* because they are false statements.

2-H   Lines 43–48 say that children understand basic grammar and can combine the meaning of several words into one word when they say things like "out" and "bottle." These are the symbolic combinations referred to in **H**. Choices **F**, **G**, and **J** exploit a potential misunderstanding of what the passage says about grammar.

3-D   "Mutually unintelligible languages" is contrasted with "same brain-generated language" in lines 68–69. The word "Instead" in line 70 sets up this contrast, suggesting that mutually unintelligible languages have few words that can be understood by speakers of different languages.

4-J   Lines 34–36 say, "The child's acquisition of the structure and meaning of language has been called the most difficult intellectual achievement in life." However, it is noted in the next sentence that most children master it easily.

5-D   Beginning in line 3, the first paragraph says that two calls were blended to make a new call and that later this call system changed to a system of sounds that could meaningfully be combined different ways. This is a description of the development of calls into language.

6-J   This question has a negative twist, asking for the choice NOT supported by the last paragraph. **F** is *stated* in lines 65–66 ("Whether this device in fact exists is not yet clear."). **G** is *stated* in lines 59–62 ("to explain the child's early acquisition and creative use of grammar . . . one set of theoreticians of grammar suggests that there may be a language acquisition device . . ."). **H** is *implied* in lines 63–65 ("As the forebrain evolved, this language acquisition device may have become part of our biological inheritance.") For **J** to be true, this device must exist. However, it is only theoretical at this point.

7-C   An open language is defined in lines 1–3: utterances combined in various ways to produce new meanings. Items **I** and **II** combine words to create meanings which are NOT represented by just one word.

8-G   To paraphrase lines 15–18, human adults changed their form of communication from calls to open language in a millennia; children change from using calls as infants to using open language in three to four years. Speaking children are compared to call-using adults.

9-B   The question asks for a skill that humans are naturally equipped for but must learn. When born, humans cannot walk but soon learn to do so as their legs and sense of balance develop naturally. Hearing normally doesn't require learning (**A**). Reading and writing are not natural, for some cultures do not have a written language (**C** and **D**).

10-H   The passage doesn't use any one culture, race, or language as an example but speaks of human language acquisition in general terms. Thus, the passage implies that language acquisition is universal.

11-D   The "habit-forming programs" are mentioned in lines 11–12, but it isn't until lines 18–22 that the author implies a connection between habit-forming television shows and the mass audience that watches for the sake of watching anything. The words "that they are there" (lines 21–22) suggest watching from habit, a characteristic of a mass audience.

12-G The main idea can be stated in many places in a passage, but it must be supported by the whole passage. Choice **G** is first suggested in lines 13–15: "But, of course . . . a declining audience need not also mean a less enthusiastic one." Then, lines 32–34 ("There has never been a larger . . . public for the kind of film which only a few years ago would have seemed desperately specialized") also suggest that the correct answer is **G**. The first paragraph begins by talking about the different names for cinema but the issue is quickly dropped (**F**). Hollywood empires declined but it is not stated that this created serious economic problems for film producers (**H**). Answer **J** is too specific; a generation having a vocabulary of the screen is only a small detail from the passage.

13-A Throughout the passage, the author uses the term "cinema" for *all* the things mentioned in **A**. **B**, **C**, and **D** are too specific. In line 23 cinema means a mass-market motion picture (**D**); in lines 35 and 50, it means an experimental film (**C**); and in line 70, it refers to European films (**B**).

14-H Paragraph 3 talks about how filmmaking was influenced by fashion. Film magazines uncover new trends and raise the viewing audience's expectations. If a director fails to fulfill a prediction set forth by these trends, that director would seem to have betrayed a promise created by fashions in the media. **F**, **G**, and **J** are not suggested by the passage.

15-B Questions such as this ask the reader to recognize what is meant by a statement in the passage. The statement is explained in the rest of the paragraph, where the reader is told that too often the public pays more attention to film fashions than to the movie (**B**). Choices **A**, **C**, and **D** contain statements that go beyond what is said in the third paragraph.

16-H Lines 78–80 describe how the studios could support a young artist like Orson Welles: "A studio could take the time to let young artists and actors develop, sure that it would still be there when the time came round to get the best out of them." Lines 80–82 describe the support he received: He was allowed to study films for the better part of a year before directing *Citizen Kane*. **F**, **G**, and **J** are not mentioned by the author in connection with Welles.

17-D An indication that a more receptive audience had evolved is found in lines 30–34 and throughout the passage. The other choices either disagree with the passage or are not supported by it. The growth of large film studios (**A**) was connected to mass-market films. Publicity about new directors (**B**) and specialization of film magazines (**C**) are treated more as potentially harmful results than causes of specialized film production.

18-F Lines 17–22 tell us that a large number of people may watch the same programs just to be watching *something*. Quality isn't always an issue. Choices **G** and **H** are directly contradictory to the information in lines 13–17. Use the true/false strategy to *ZAP* **J** because of the word "always."

19-C Lines 15–17 say: "The Pilkington Report, in another context, has nailed the fallacy of claiming to gauge public taste on a purely statistical basis." There is no evidence that the report discussed either movies or television **A**, **B**, and **D**. It is made clear that it pointed out the shortcomings of relating statistical evidence to matters of taste.

20-J Overall, the author had positive and negative things to say about the evolution of cinema. After speaking of "heavy casualties" in line 72, she describes how the large studio system could afford to let an artist develop, but that "this could hardly happen now" (lines 82–83). When you see these different viewpoints, you can conclude that the author has mixed feelings about the change in cinema over the years.

Reading Answer Review
Workout C

1-C   C is a recurring theme in each of the five paragraphs. The other choices are too specific to be the main topic. The first paragraph talks about how stars "burn" (**A**), but then explains the role of gravity. The force that binds atoms (**B**) is discussed only in the first paragraph and how gas clouds are formed (**D**) is discussed only in the second paragraph.

2-G   It is important to note that this question is asking for the *second* most common element, which is helium (lines 54–55).

3-A   Lines 69–72 say that the shrinking of a gas cloud is referred to as a collapse. The word collapse implies that the contraction is sudden and rapid.

4-J   The context of lines 11–15 compares "profound" to "superficial." Superficial refers to chemical reactions that do not alter the basic nature of the atom. When nuclear reactions are said to be profound, it means that they alter the basic nature of the atom.

5-A   The first sentence states "a star burns only in the sense that it . . . gives off light somewhat the way a flame of a match . . . gives off light." The rest of the paragraph contrasts a candle's flame to a star's release of energy.

6-F   The passage explains that stars are formed when gravity pulls the particles in gas clouds together. Thus, all stars began as gas clouds.

7-B   This question has a negative twist, asking which would NOT result in a gas cloud's forming into a star. Lines 62–63 say that if the particles of a gas cloud are "moving fast enough, they may disperse before they can fall together."

8-J   Lines 18–20 say, "In the centers of stars . . . the atoms are pressed together so hard that the nuclei hit each other." Since the atoms in the center are pressed together more than the atoms toward the outside, the centers are more dense.

9-D   Gravity is defined in lines 24–26 as the force that makes all particles of matter in the universe attract all other particles. Lines 38–39 attribute this discovery to Isaac Newton.

10-F   Lines 20–21 say "a star's heat comes from nuclear reactions"—or the nuclei of atoms hitting each other. A nuclear reactor also creates heat through the collisions of subatomic particles.

11-A   Lines 51–52 tell what Cortes described: ". . . the dishes at Montezuma's table as being of four classes: meat, fish, herbs and fruit." Cortes and his soldier Bernal Diaz del Castillo are cited in lines 76–82: "They both described the banquets . . ." None of the details in the other choices are suggested by the passage.

12-J   Lines 4–6 say six and a half millennia (6,500 years) before the first Spaniard set foot in the New World (which is in the early 1,500s), the "humans that hunted and gathered . . . began to settle into agricultural ways."

13-B   The question requires that you read lines 69–71: "it (the market at Tenochtitlan) sounds not unlike the aggressively sensual offerings in and around the colossal Merced market at the center of present-day Mexico City."

14-J   "Myriad" means "many." The whole passage described the variety of Aztec foods. "Myriad" is used to describe the dishes of the ruling class. One can expect that they would have a great variety available.

15-B   **I** is not suggested by the passage; although the author describes a complex society, he or she does not hint that it was more sophisticated than modern cultures. **III** is false; the Spaniards found many unfamiliar foods upon their arrival in the New World. This means you can *ZAP* **A**, **C**, and **D**. **B**, the only choice left, is supported by the subject matter of the passage.

16-H   Lines 13–15 mention the development of corn and describe corn as one of the builders and sustainers of American civilization. Lines 13–14 say corn was developed 1,000 or 2,000 years after the early Americans settled into agricultural camps. The passage doesn't mention whether or not corn was traded with the Spaniards (**F**) and corn was developed before the Spanish arrived (**G**). Cattle and dairy farming was never mentioned as a part of pre-Spanish Mexico (**J**).

17-C   Reread paragraph 5. The words "top-heavy domination" suggest that this "far and wide" Aztec rule was unstable. The conquered people of the empire, or "everyday people" as described in the passage, had to live off of a simple diet of atole, beans, and tortillas, which was barely enough to sustain them. The common people could not afford to let their lives get worse. If famine struck, they would have to rebel against the Aztec rule that had led to the famine.

18-G   Lines 36–37 mention that atole was the staple food of the everyday people. The noble class would NOT serve the food of the everyday people at their banquets.

19-B   A part of analytical reading is determining the source of the information in a passage. Three names of Europeans are mentioned throughout the passage, so we can deduce that the information came from these people: Hernan Cortes, lines 51 and 67; Friar Sahagún, line 53; and Bernal Díaz del Castillo, line 77.

20-J   In lines 59–61, tomato sauce is mentioned as part of Friar Sahagun's detailed description of early Aztec society. One of the two commonly used sauces is like a tomato sauce, depending on how much chile or tomato a cook would put in it.

Reading Answer Review
Workout D

1-D   The first two paragraphs introduce the reader to the town, Miss Emily, her house, and her death. The remaining four paragraphs describe an incident that occurred as a result of Miss Emily's refusal to pay taxes.

2-F   Lines 27–30 say, "Colonel Sartoris invented an involved tale to the effect that Miss Emily's father had loaned money to the town, which the town . . . preferred this way of repaying."

3-C   The answer is in the second paragraph, which begins by saying the house had once been located on the town's "most select street" and then describes the gradual decay of that neighborhood.

4-H   A clue to the meaning of "archaic" can be found in the character of Miss Emily. She is a recluse in an ancient house. She refuses to keep up with the times. It would be consistent with all we know about her for her handwriting to be old-fashioned.

5-B   You know Miss Emily would not have asked for assistance (lines 26–27), so you can *ZAP* **A**. It says that Colonel Sartoris made up the story about Miss Emily's father lending money to the town, so you can *ZAP* **C**. There is no evidence that the town wanted to preserve her house, so you can *ZAP* **D**. It is reasonable to infer, however, that Colonel Sartoris and the townspeople valued her. **B** is the correct choice.

6-H   The question asks how we, the readers, know that the whole town thought Miss Emily was an eccentric. The only clue we have is that the whole town went to her funeral. The rest of the choices do not demonstrate that the townspeople found her eccentric, only that she was eccentric.

7-D   In fiction, a person's character is often revealed in the way that person behaves and the way he/she relates to others. Physical appearance is important, but not as important as descriptions that show how a character behaved and thought, and what others thought of that character. **A** hints at what the town thought of her. **B** and **C** show her actions. Her physical appearance (**D**) does the least to tell the reader who Miss Emily was.

8-J   The passage reveals that the town officials visited Miss Emily at some point. The first paragraph gives a clue to when this visit took place. Lines 4–6 say, "the inside of her house, which no one save [except] an old manservant . . . had seen in at least ten years."

9-B   If the later generation had accepted that Colonel Sartoris had the right to exempt Miss Emily from the town laws, the town officials never would have visited her. **A** is unlikely because nothing in the passage suggests that the new town officials wouldn't support poor individuals. **C** is not correct, because they were being respectful of Miss Emily by writing her and offering to give her a ride to the sheriff's office. **D** is not mentioned at all in the passage.

10-G   The narrator refers to "*our* whole town" (line 1) as though he lived there.

11-D   The main idea will be the effect of the whole passage and not the effect of just one or two paragraphs. **B** and **C** are discussed in the passage, but we read about them as the author is describing a greater subject—the development of professional lawyers. **A** is not supported by the passage.

12-H   Lines 17–23 say oratory began in the fifth century B.C.

13-B   *Rhetores* are discussed in lines 23–28. They are said to have begun the "fateful change" from a society without lawyers to a society with lawyers. This occurred in the fifth century B.C. Next, lines 56–61 say the *logographoi* came into existence in the fourth century B.C. Lines 67–72 describe the step to "full-fledged professional lawyering" as having followed the Greek *logographoi*.

14-G   The commentary on wile and guile is in the sentences that follow lines 43–44. They describe a character who tries to cheat his creditors, a "lawbook on legs, who can snoop like a beagle, a double-faced, lethal-tongued eagle." "Craftiness" most closely resembles this description.

15-D   Lines 77–78 say "these *juris prudentes* . . . rarely took cases and when they did, they received no fee. Their chief concern was analysis of the law." This is most like a modern law professor.

16-J   Lines 29–32 say that the speaker's dais (or podium) was as important to their politicians as television is to our politicians today. Apparently, the medium for giving speeches has changed but the necessity to give speeches hasn't.

17-C   Lines 38–41 say that Aristophanes satirized the goings-on of the rhetores. Lines 31–32 tell us that the *rhetores* were involved in legal coaching.

18-F   The passage views lawyers in terms of their history. The history of lawyering shows the development of the art of persuasion. The passage as a whole, focuses on how the art of persuasion has developed into the modern law profession.

19-A   Look at the first paragraph. The author is initially stating an opinion, but notice the rest of the passage presents facts from history. **B**, **C**, and **D** are from this part of the passage.

20-H   Lines 82–84 describe advocati as people who are only summoned to one's side to provide legal advice. Lines 87–89 say that *causidici* were speakers of cases, often speaking entirely for the client.

Reading Answer Review
Workout E

1-D   Choosing a central theme calls for you to consider the whole passage and select an answer choice which best states its meaning. This passage is more about prey behavior than predator behavior, so **B** and **C** are wrong because they give predators either greater or equal importance. **A** is wrong because the passage deals with many prey behaviors besides the protection of nesting sites. **D** is correct because it states clearly that the passage is about the behavior of prey.

2-F   To answer correctly, you must find or remember a detail from lines 37–39: ". . . Eastern Meadowlarks . . . are generally immune to aerial predators,". . . The falcon is an aerial predator. Raccoons, humans, and snakes are not.

3-D   In line 50 you see the phrase "sitting close" and must deduce its meaning from the context. The surrounding paragraph says birds that rely on camouflage are good at sitting close, which means staying very still. Camouflage is an attempt to blend in with the surroundings. A moving animal (one not sitting close) would be easy to see, and an animal that is sitting close would be hard to see.

4-J   You must deduce the meaning of "histrionics" from the context of the whole paragraph. Lines 61–67 describe how the Killdeer *pretends* that it has a broken wing. It is trying to look vulnerable when in fact it is quite capable of flying away. You need to deduce that "histrionics" refers to the bird's acting performance: an attempt to fake that its wing is broken.

5-B   The question requires that you understand the effect of the Killdeer's behavior on the predator. It is clear from the expression "easy catch" (line 66) that the bird's actions convince the predator that the Killdeer cannot protect itself from an attack.

6-J   This question requires that you understand the relationship between the evolving behavior of the two species. Then you must paraphrase the sentence in lines 9–10: "Sparrows have made Sharp-shinned Hawks swift . . ." Sharp-shinned hawks wouldn't be as fast, or swift, if not for the cautiousness of sparrows.

7-A   The question asks the reader to generalize about anti-predator behavior. **A** is general enough to cover all anti-predator behavior described in the passage and not so specific in that it describes only some of the birds. All of the birds described in the passage have in some way adapted to special circumstances; for example, the Gray Gull has adapted to life in the desert; the Sora has developed an appearance that resembles its hiding place among cattails. Answer choices **B** and **C** are too specific, and **D** is too general.

8-G   The Gray Gull of Chile nests in the desert (lines 14–15). The paragraph goes on to say that its predators avoid such an inhospitable place. The desert is uncomfortable yet the Gray Gull chooses to nest there. lines 21–22 say that most birds can't do this, so it is incorrect to say that more species could (**F**). Nothing is said about how fast the Gray Gull flies (**H**). Nor is it said that the Gull's predators couldn't survive a similar flight (**J**).

9-C   The anti-predator behaviors described in the passage fall into three categories: avoidance, camouflage, and distraction. All three are used to avoid predators (**A**). All can be used to either protect young (**B**) or work against a single predator (**D**). Distraction displays are the only strategies that attempt to gain the predator's attention.

10-H The American Bittern is mentioned in line 44 as a bird that uses camouflage. Camouflage (blending in visually with the surroundings) makes an animal hard to see. Camouflage does not hide the smell of an animal, and so the Bittern would be vulnerable to predators that hunt by sense of smell. **F**, **G**, and **J** all suggest predators that use their sight for hunting.

11-A   Lines 44–45 say, "it was generally the idea or concept of the animal which the artist expressed." **B** is not true because lines 64–66 imply that the carvings could be very realistic. There is no evidence that the artists had to obey any religious rules (**C**). **D** is not true because lines 28–29 say that the relationship between man and certain animals was intimate.

12-H   Lines 14–15 suggest that a Northwest Coat object is easily recognized. Lines 17–19 explain that established designs are repeated over and over. These established designs, which are later described as the heritage of the culture, are what make Northwest Coast Indian art easy to recognize.

13-B   Lines 9–12 say "Even when his products were made to serve practical purposes, the shapes and decorations were devised to have meaning; and even further, a meaning that would enhance the use of the product."

14-G   Lines 40–42 describe "the line of demarcation" between men and animals as being "slight." Since the passage suggests many times the strong connection between humans and animals, it makes sense that the line of "separation" is slight.

15-C   Lines 24–27 say: "The world was seen by the Northwest Coast Indian as the habitation of a multiplicity of spirits in which the human spirit slips almost imperceptibly into those of various animals, and vice versa."

16-H   Line 66 suggests that the eyes give the carving a sense of having inner life.

17-B   One way to solve this type of problem is to check each foil and *ZAP* those which seem most clearly "suggested" by the passage. Choice **A** is strongly supported. *ZAP* it. Choice **B** is questionable—leave it. Choice **C** is somewhat difficult because the passage doesn't state directly that the animals were well known. However since the animals are beavers, whales, etc . . . , there is the "suggestion" that they are well known. *ZAP* **C**. Now the choice is between **B** and **D**. There seems to be more support in the passage for **D** than **B**, so **B** is the answer.

18-H   This question has a negative twist, asking which item is LEAST likely to be a Northwest Coast Indian artifact. The art of the Northwest Coast Indian emphasized animal and human features represented either as symbols or realistic figures. **H** is the only choice that omits the human or animal element.

19-D   Lines 73–75 say that the identities of the figures in a piece of art may have been known only to the man for whom it was made and the man who made it.

20-J   This question asks you to infer something that is NOT stated but is implied in the passage. **F** is wrong; while the author does try demonstrate the depth of meaning behind the art, he is not saying that it is the most beautiful Native American art. **G** is wrong, because the author does not imply that the Northwest Coast Indians were closer to nature than other Native American cultures. **H** is wrong, because the passage only discusses the art of the Northwest Coast Indians. **J** is the only reasonable inference you can make.

Reading Answer Review
Workout F

1-A   Each of the four choices suggests troubled family relations and is found in the passage. The mention of divorce (line 6) comes first, followed by **D** (lines 16–20), **B** (lines 31 and 34), and **C** (line 35).

2-F   Line 1 says, "My father stands in the kitchen . . ." and line 7 says, "I stand in the doorway, watching him do dishes." Al doesn't enter the kitchen until after the conversation begins.

3-B   Lines 16–17 say, "For the last several years, I have felt peculiar around my father . . ."

4-J   The clue to the meaning of "derisive" is Al's attitude throughout the passage. Al is trying to make his father believe that he doesn't care about his opinion or the track team. Under these circumstances, he would most likely try to make his laugh sound mocking.

5-A   This question asks for a probable reason, so you need to see which answer is likely and compare it to those that are definitely not supported by the passage. We know that Al seems to be unhappy, and he is annoyed by the coach's efforts to recruit him, so it is likely that he wants to avoid group activities (**A**). There is no evidence that he quarreled with other runners (**B**). He doesn't mention that he wants to spend more time with his father or join the team (**C**). Since the coach has apparently seen him running, there is no reason to assume he dislikes it (**D**).

6-H   Al reflects three times on the trouble he has communicating with his father: lines 18–19 ("I don't like to be alone with him. I don't know what to say."); lines 70–71 ("Sometimes I think I'd like him better if we did yell at each other."); and lines 73–74 ("I stop, look at the floor. Perhaps my voice is too sharp, full of the same bitterness as his."). None of the other choices is supported by the passage.

7-C   The frustration of Al's father is suggested in lines 56–58, when he says, "Would it compromise you that much to join something, once in your life?"

8-F   Line 35 ("Sometimes I hate my father for his sarcasm.") refers to his remark "One of your pals from school" in line 31. There is no evidence that the other choices are sarcastic.

9-C   Al compares his face to his parents in lines 47–49. The words "strong," "cold," and "arrogant" do more than describe a face; they describe the person behind the face.

10-G   Once Al discovers that his father has spoken with the coach, he becomes resentful and withdrawn. In lines 36–37, he does not answer his father immediately, and in line 43 he refers to the coach's remarks as "crap."

11-A   Lines 66–68 say "*Noh's* appeal is limited, since its form was fixed long ago. The language, based on aristocratic speech of the fourteenth century, is unintelligible to most people today."

12-H   Lines 3–5 say "When Buddhism was introduced into Japan during the sixth century A.D., dance plays set to music came with it."

13-A   Lines 11–15 say that both *dengaku* and *sarugaku* "were medleys of disconnected songs, dances, and short sketches." Short sketches are considered theater.

14-G   The sentence says the majority of lines were sung or intoned, and few were spoken. From this sentence you can deduce that the meaning of "intoned" is similar to "sung." Of the choices, chanting is most similar to singing.

15-D   The best clue is in lines 29–32 which say that Japan's middle ages had a new political and social structure, and that art was flourishing. This description rules out **A** (being ruled by China), **B** (where art only served the emperor), and **C** (where the society was politically unstable).

16-F   Lines 13–14 say that *sarugaku* grew out of ritualistic elements imported from China, and lines 15–17 say that *Noh* evolved out of *sarugaku*. Thus, Noh developed from ritual entertainments that came from China, and lines 3–5 suggest that these entertainments were influenced by Buddhism.

17-A   Lines 5–9 say that the right to perform *bugaku* is passed down through generations of families with hereditary rights to the art form.

18-H   Lines 19–20 say "*Noh* reached its highest point with Kannami's son, Zeami Motokiyo (1363–1443)." The fourteenth and fifteenth centuries are the years following 1300 and 1400.

19-B   Lines 66–67 say that Noh's form "was fixed long ago." You can ZAP **A** because Japanese theater flourished during the period of the Shogunate. You can ZAP **C** because there is no evidence that Zeami's innovations caused Noh plays to gain acceptance. You can ZAP **D** because lines 55–56 say that Noh's language is "unintelligible to most persons today." That leaves **B**.

20-G   Lines 50–56 talk about Buddhist influence on *Noh*. They say that Zeami adopted the conviction that beauty lies in suggestion, simplicity, subtlety, and restraint.

Science Answer Review
Workout A

Passage I (Research Summary)

1-D The holding tank of System 1 starts out warmer because both experiments show System 1 losing heat between Points A and B. We can deduce that System 2 is always colder than System 1 because in both experiments, System 2 gains heat between Points C and D. Since Points A and B show a lower temperature, cooling takes place in the exchange tank (so **III** is true). This means that cooler water is being returned to the holding tank of System 1 and warmer water is being returned to System 2. Cooling must also take place in the holding tank of System 2 for it to remain 20°C when warmed water is entering it from the exchange tank.

2-J The only difference between the two experiments is the direction of water flow in System 1. To compare this you need to conduct trials in which you vary the direction of water flow. Each experiment by itself compares copper pipe to glass (**H**) using different sizes (**F**) and different types of pipe (**G**); so each experiment by itself is enough to answer whether size and type of pipe affects heat exchange.

3-B Looking at the chart for Experiment 1, the temperature at Point D for 1" glass pipe is 21°C and for 2" glass pipe is 23°C. If the pipe were 3" wide, it is likely that the temperature would increase another 2°C, giving a reading of 23°C.

4-F Energy is neither created nor destroyed, and therefore, the missing heat energy must be lost to the surroundings. Most of the exposure to the surroundings occurs around the large exchange tank, so insulating this tank would lessen the exposure and keep the heat within the apparatus of the experiment.

5-C The passage explains that pumps are in both systems, so **D** can be eliminated. You can figure out that a heater is required because if System 1 loses heat as its water flows through the exchange tank, then that heat must be replenished by a heater to keep the holding tank at 60°C.

6-F If the liquid of System 1 flows more slowly, it will have more time to cool, so the temperature at the exit point (Point A) would be lower.

Passage II (Data Representation)

Figure 1 is a graph with six shapes used to represent quantities. The wider a vertical cross section is, the greater quantity it indicates. The figures are divided into three ages of a lake: young, mature, and old. To better illustrate the three phases, the figures have gray, white, and black portions. The information is not about one specific lake; it is based on the study of many lakes.

7-D The key words in the question are "total number of organisms." The top shape in Figure 1 represents the total number of organisms. Beginning at the left, the shape gradually gets wider during the young portion, remains the same during the mature age, and then swells during old age. **D** is the only answer that describes this relationship.

8-G The bottom of Figure 1 shows "Lake Age" between two arrows. Graphs usually have the horizontal or vertical directions labeled. The horizontal labeling is usually at the bottom but can also appear at the top. The vertical labeling can be on the right or the left of the graph.

9-A This question requires that you compare one shape (rate of nutrient recycling) to the horizontal axis (which shows the age of the lake). The words "rate of nutrient recycling" call your attention to the second shape from the top. You do not need to know what "nutrient recycling" means, but rather, how to interpret the shape. Since the shape gets wider from left to right, the rate goes up as the lake gets older.

10-G   Information can be represented in different ways. Figure 1 has information represented visually. Of Graphs I, II, III, and IV, only one correctly represents the relationship between lake age and variety of life. Graph II shows a sharp increase, followed by a long stable period, and then a sharp decrease. Graph I begins with a decrease. Graphs III and IV begin with an increase and never decrease.

11-C   To answer this question, you need to look at the bottom two shapes of Figure 1 and find any place where the two shapes have the same width. Next, you determine which of statements I, II, and III are true and which are false. I is true, so every possible correct answer will have I in it; thus, you can *ZAP* **D**. II is false, so you can *ZAP* **B**. III is true, so you can *ZAP* **A**.

Passage III (Conflicting Viewpoints)

12-F   The first paragraph explains that both groups of scientists are trying to explain why so many species became extinct at the end of the Cretaceous Period. Therefore, both groups accept **F**, that many large animals species had become extinct.

13-C   Group 1 claims that a chain reaction from a meteor impact caused winters hostile enough to kill the dinosaurs. Group 2 refutes this by saying that dinosaurs on the Australian continent were already subject to, and therefore surviving, the kind of winter resulting from a meteor collision. This assumption overlooks the possibility that winter-like conditions caused by a meteor collision could make a normal winter exceptionally harsh.

14-H   The scientists of Group 1 need to find proof of two things to support that their theory is a viable cause of mass extinctions and therefore can be applied to other mass extinctions: 1) proof of a meteor collision at the end of the Cretaceous; and 2) proof that dust thrown up from a meteor collision could cause a catastrophic global winter. **H** is possible proof that a meteor did strike at the end of the Permian. Knowing this, Group 1 could argue that the causes of the Permian and Cretaceous extinctions were similar.

15-B   Group 1 needs to prove that dust thrown up from a meteor collision could create a global winter. **B** is correct because forest fires also produce a lot of smoke and dust. If these could lower global temperatures, then it is very likely that a much greater disaster, like a meteor collision, could lower temperatures enough to create a global winter.

16-G   The last sentence of the passage says that Group 2 believes that the mass extinction by the end of the Cretaceous Period was gradual. Only Line **G** shows a gradual decline in numbers. Incidentally, Line **H** represents Group 1's theory of sudden mass extinction at the end of the Cretaceous Period.

17-A   Group 1 insists that all dinosaurs were wiped out by the mass extinction. This would include the dinosaurs of the Australian continent which Group 2 admits were extinct by the end of the Cretaceous. This means that the Australian dinosaurs could have been killed as a result of Group 1's meteor impact.

18-F   Group 1's theory is that meteoric dust and debris filtered out the sunlight, killing plant life and the dinosaurs. A new discovery of deposits left by an extraterrestrial object adds nothing to this theory.

Science Answer Review
Workout B

Passage I (Research Summary)

Experiments 1 and 2 are attempts to study the relationship between magnetism, motion, and electricity. The first experiment establishes that electricity is generated when a magnet moves through a wire. Experiment 2 determines how the speed of the magnet affects the amount of electricity produced.

1-C   Experiment 1 is *qualitative* because it deals with what qualities are discovered when you pass a magnet through a wire coil. It was discovered that passing a magnet through a coil of wire produces electricity. Experiment 2 is *quantitative* because it determines what quantities of electricity are produced. For example, 4.43 amperes is the quantity produced when the magnet is allowed to freely fall through the coil.

2-H   The diagram of Experiment 1 shows the magnet on a string that is fed through two pulleys, and a weight on the other end of the string on a hook. The more weight you add to the hook, the slower the magnet will fall.

3-B   The chart shows how much electricity is produced using different weights on the hook. The heavier the weight, the slower the magnet moves through the coil. Since the greatest weight (0.8 kg) resulted in the least amperes, and the least weight (no weight added), yielded the greatest amperes, you can deduce that the faster the velocity (or speed) of the magnet, the greater the current generated will be.

4-J   A change in the distance between the pulleys will not change the effect of gravity on the falling magnet.

5-D   The weights on the hook are an attempt to regulate how fast the magnet falls through the hoop. By using the same weight, the experiment is consistent. Every time the magnet falls through the hoop with a .4 kg weight, the experimenter knows that the magnet is falling at the same rate of speed. However, the experimenter doesn't know exactly how fast the magnet is falling the moment it enters the hoop. Knowing how fast the magnet was falling each time will improve the data.

6-F   Power plants generate electricity by spinning huge coils through powerful magnetic fields at great speeds. Experiments 1 and 2 also generate electricity but on a much smaller scale. Since the experiment took place on the earth, we can conclude that it was not measurably affected by electrical fields in the earth and has little value for measuring such fields (**G**). Understanding how certain materials conduct electricity can be done with a more reliable (or consistent) power source, such as a battery (**H**). Devising a theory of magnetism would involve much more attention to how the magnet works than was shown in Experiments 1 and 2.

Passage II (Data Representation)

Graphs A, B, and C show the correlation between the increase of greenhouse gases (CO_2 and methane) over the years 1850 and 1990 and the increase in average temperatures for those same years. Graph A has a horizontal line drawn through the middle that represents the average temperature measured between 1950 and 1980. Note that the years are labeled in 20-year intervals and that CO_2 is carbon dioxide.

7-D You need to examine each answer and see if it corresponds to increases and decreases on the graphs. Only Graphs B and C show increases. Since the question has a negative twist, asking which does NOT show an increase, you must look at Graph A where decreases in mean temperatures are shown for the years 1900–1910, 1940–1950, and 1955–1970. Only 1900–1910 is offered as an answer.

8-H The mean temperatures for each of the years sampled are represented by the dots and NOT by the curved line. The vertical line between 1910 and 1930 stands for 1920, where a dot is the closest of the four choices to the horizontal line representing the mean temperature between 1950 and 1980.

9-C The curved lines do not represent data but assumptions and trends. You need to compare the answer choices to the places they refer to on the graphs and find years cited in the four answer choices that do not have any dots plotted. Graph C, representing methane, shows no dots between 1960 and 1970.

10-J Looking at Graph G you see that the concentration of CO_2 was greater in 1980 than in 1850, so the correct answer will show the dark bar as being greater. This eliminates answers **G** and **H** where the light bar for 1850 is greater. Answer **F** is tempting because Graph G places the concentration in 1980 several times higher than 1850. It is important to realize that the bottom of Graph G begins at 280 parts per million. If Graph G were drawn so that it started at 0 parts per million, the difference between 1850 and 1980 would look like the bar graph in **J**. It's as though the graphs have only enough room for the tips of the icebergs.

11-C On all three graphs, the lines drawn among the points indicate trends. You need to follow the line for each and extend it to the end of each graph. Graph A would show .15 deviation from the 1950–80 mean; Graph B, 360 ppm CO_2; and Graph C, 1.75 ppm methane.

Passage III (Research Summary)

12-H You need to examine each of the four choices, deciding which conclusion is true and which three are false. When the decreased diameter was lowered one meter in Experiment 3, the water pressure increased. Answers **F** and **G** are wrong because each implies that narrowing the tube and lowering the tube had the same effect on water pressure. In truth, narrowing the tube decreased the pressure and lowering the tube increased the pressure. **H** is correct because a decrease in diameter caused the water pressure in the narrow part of the tube to decrease (Experiment 2). **J** is wrong; although the two factors had opposite effects on water pressure, the lowered elevation did not cancel out the effect of the narrowed tube.

13-D This is a question that can be answered using common sense. **A** can be *ZAPPED* because there is no reason to assume that the air pressure outside each of the three vertical tubes is different. **B** and **C** can be *ZAPPED* because the volume of the water in the tube neither increases nor decreases at any point. **D** is the only choice left.

14-J We are told that the fluid pressure in the middle tube is the lowest of the three. We are also told that the velocity is higher in the middle tube. The only answer that expresses this relationship is **J**: As the velocity increases, fluid pressure decreases.

15-B   The answer can be found by taking the difference between the water levels for the middle tube of the second and third experiments:

30 cm − 22.5 cm = 7.5 cm

16-G   The hypothetical experiment is like Experiment 3, except that the glass tube is raised a meter instead of lowered a meter. When the tube was lowered one meter, the water level rose 7.5 cm; if the tube were raised one meter, the water level should decrease by 7.5 cm.

22.5 − 7.5 = 15 cm

17-A   Capping the tubes stops the water flow. As a result, the fluid velocity is irrelevant. Since the atmospheric pressure and the fluid volume would remain constant, the answer is **A**.

Passage IV (Data Representation)

18-J   The question asks for a microorganism that has increased by a power 10^2 over 2 days. **A** and **B** increase on the first day. However, by the second day the numbers decrease so the total after 2 days shows less than a 10^2 increase. **C** shows a 10^1 increase. **D** increases steadily over a 2 day period.

19-B   This question requires that you look at one graph (salmonellae for ham salad) and find the part of the graph that shows the greatest upward increase. This occurs between days 1 and 2 at 95°F.

20-H   As in question 37, you must look at one chart (salmonellae for chicken a la king) and find the graph between days 1 and 2 to see which line shows the greatest upward increase. This occurs at 50°F.

21-B   The experiment reveals only the growth rates of salmonellae and staphylococci when stored at various temperatures up to 5 days. Answers **A**, **C**, and **D** all assume that a low growth rate of these bacteria means the food is safe. A safe level of bacteria is not given in this experiment.

22-J   Neither graph shows the results past the fifth day, so you will have to project the graphs following their direction. The graphs that show potential increases are 44°F, 46°F, and 48°F for chicken a la king. Of these, 44°F begins with the greatest number. It is likely that after a sixth day, 48°F will continue to have the most salmonellae.

Science Answer Review
Workout C

Passage I (Conflicting Viewpoints)

Your clue that this passage is the one on conflicting viewpoints is that the opinions of two people are represented in the paragraphs labeled Geologist 1 and Geologist 2. A viewpoint can only be present where there are people cited and viewpoints cannot conflict unless there is more than one person involved.

1-B   Geologist 1 supports his statement that there are no deep earthquakes by saying that the techniques for measuring earthquakes are inaccurate. However, he has no proof of this. Answer **B** would be the proof he needs that the measurements were inaccurate.

2-J   This question has a negative twist in the word "contradict," so you need to look for the statement that definitely has a negative effect on Geologist 1's theory. Geologist 1 insists that "the earth is plastic below a depth of from 60 to 100 kilometers and *cannot fracture*." **J** contradicts this assertion, suggesting that asthenosphere can break like a brittle solid.

3-A   Geologist 2 claims that deep earthquakes are caused by plates of lithosphere that have been pushed down into the asthenosphere by other plates of lithosphere. This could only happen where at least two lithosphere plates intersect.

4-G   The second paragraph says that seismic data collected over 85 years suggest that earthquakes have occurred at depths above 50 to over 600 km. Although it isn't stated, we can assume that most scientists do not dispute this 85 years worth of data. Geologist 1 claims that this data is wrong because it doesn't work with his theory. This is not a good enough reason to reject 85 years of data.

5-B   Graph II is the only graph suggesting that no earthquakes occur at depths lower than 100 km. According to Geologist 1, there should be no earthquakes below 100 km because material that deep is plastic and cannot fracture.

6-H   Geologist 1 insists that ALL material in the asthenosphere is plastic-like and flexible. Geologist 1 does not state that lithosphere can be in the asthenosphere. For lithosphere to be in the asthenosphere, then this lithosphere must become plastic-like. According to Geologist 1, the same forces that make the asthenosphere plastic-like, would also affect any plates of lithosphere that got into the asthenosphere.

7-B   The asthenosphere is described as plastic-like by both geologists. In this use, "plastic" means that it can be molded and bent. This allows the asthenosphere to alter its shape.

Passage II (Research Summary)

8-J This control group should experience the same conditions as the experimental group except for the injections. This includes meals. All rats should have the same diet.

9-D Group B shows that streptozotocin induces symptoms that resemble diabetes. Group C also received streptozoticin, but didn't show the same symptoms because they also received insulin. The insulin given to Group C reduced the symptoms shown in Group B.

10-G This question closely resembles the previous question. Group A is the control group—normal rats showing no symptoms and receiving no drugs. Group C received drugs to induce diabetes-like symptoms but had these symptoms reduced by another drug.

11-D If the effect of streptozotocin on rats resembles that of diabetes in humans, then the data in the chart show three symptoms: loss of weight, increase in blood sugar, and decrease in the size of fat cells. Only loss of weight is offered as an answer.

12-G The rats of Group B show the strongest symptoms of diabetes and were injected with streptozotocin only.

13-C The symptoms of diabetes in rats (loss of weight and increase in blood sugar) were accompanied by a decrease in the average size of fat cells. The change in fat cells in humans would be a useful and logical relationship to study.

Passage III (Data Representation)

14-G The column "Salt Filtered from the Water" shows how much of each salt did NOT dissolve. All 10 grams of the sodium chloride sample dissolved, while only 0.5 grams of silver chloride and 1.4 grams of barium nitrate dissolved. Therefore, sodium chloride is more soluble than the other two salts.

15-C The problem with the experiment is that we don't know how wet each of the three salts was before it was put in water. To even this out, you need to make sure that the three salt samples are equally wet. Recovering undissolved salts from water is the simplest way to ensure that each is equally wet.

16-F To compute the solubility of silver chloride, you must subtract 9.5 grams (filtered from the water) from the original amount of 10 grams. 0.5 grams dissolved in 1 liter of water, so the solubility of silver chloride is 0.5 grams per liter.

17-A If sodium chloride is 20 times as soluble as barium nitrate, multiply 20 times the solubility of barium nitrate to get the solubility of sodium chloride.

solubility of barium nitrate = 1.4 grams per liter
× 2 0

solubility of sodium chloride = 2 8 grams per liter

So, if 20 grams of sodium chloride was added to 1 liter of water, all of it would dissolve with 0 grams recovered.

18-H Since solubility is determined by how many grams dissolve per liter of water, this rate will not change when less water is used. Less salt will dissolve in less water, but the amount per liter will remain constant.

Science Answer Review
Workout D

Passage I (Data Representation)

1-A   This question has a negative twist, asking which is NOT supported. This type of question often requires that you examine each answer choice against the chart and see which are true and which are not. **A** is not supported; males and females both spend a lot of time foraging (brick, gray) as shown on the chart. **B** is supported because male traveling (black) is larger in most columns than female traveling (zigzag). **C** is supported because resting (slash) is smaller in most columns for males than for females. **D** is supported because female foraging (brick) is smallest during the afternoon.

2-F   This question has a negative twist, asking during which hour the chimpanzees are least likely to be resting. The symbol (slash) which indicates time spent resting for males and females, is the smallest in the column representing 0700.

3-D   If you look at the column for 1500, you will see that female foraging is less than male foraging. The same is true at 1600: females foraged less than males. At 1700, females foraged more; at 1800, females and males foraged the same amount of time. On the graphs, the male behavior is graphed as a straight, horizontal line, and the segmented line shows whether females did more or less than the males for each time period. If you keep in mind "less, less, more, same," you will see that only IV shows the female graph to be less, less, more, same for the four hours plotted.

4-J   Where the activity patterns are similar—meaning that the chimpanzees spent the same amount of time traveling, resting, and foraging—the graphs for males and females appear the same. Above 1800, the graphs for males and females are identical.

5-C   For this question you need to examine each of the answer choices, determining true from false conclusions. **A** is false because resting (slash) only decreases during the afternoon for males. **B** is false because foraging (brick, gray) increases significantly during the afternoon for males only. **C** is true. **D** is false because foraging (brick) decreases during the afternoon for females between 1200 and 1500.

Passage II (Research Summary)

6-H   According to the chart for endothelial cells (Results of Experiment 1), the highest concentration of histamine is 10^{-3} and the amount of HRP taken up at this concentration is 6.00 micrograms. Note that with negative exponents, 10^{-3} is greater than 10^{-4}.

7-B   As the concentration of histamine increases from 0 to 10^{-3} micrograms per milliliter, the amount of protein absorbed by the two types of cells increases. This is a positive effect: an increase in histamine causes an increase in HRP being taken up.

8-G   Experiments 1 and 2 show that histamines have an effect on how much HRP is taken up by cells. However, HRPs are not mentioned in the descriptive information as having any relationship with hardening of the arteries. The first sentence explains that lipids are involved. The scientist is assuming that HRP and lipids are taken up by cells in the same way.

9-D   You need to find on each graph two levels of HRP that are close in quantity. 6.00 for endothelial cells and 5.80 for smooth muscle cells are closest, and their histamine concentrations are 10^{-3} and 10^{-4}.

10-F The question requires that you look at the values for 0 histamine concentration in both charts. After each, some concentration of histamine was found.

11-D In each case for this question you need to examine each answer choice and see if it is supported by the data. Since the question has a negative twist in asking which is NOT supported, it helps to label the answers true or false as you go through them. **A** is true. Values of HRP found in smooth muscle cells are greater for equal concentrations of histamine. **B** is true. Compare 1.12 for 0 histamine and 2.63 for 10^{-6}. **C** is true: Permeability means the ability of a cell to be penetrated. If the cell walls were not permeable, then HRP wouldn't be able to get in at all. Since greater levels of HRP are found when histamine is used, histamine increases the permeability. **D** is false because the charts show that smooth muscle cells take up more HRP than endothelial cells, not less. Compare 1.12 for smooth muscle cells and 0.16 for endothelial cells.

Passage III (Research Summary)

12-J Figure 1 shows the following results of Experiment 1: as time passed, fewer bacteria survived, so time may have had an effect. Higher temperatures made the number of survivors smaller, so temperature may have had an effect. And, since agent X was applied to ALL tests in Experiment 1, we don't know if it had an effect or not. We can only assume that agent X may have affected the survival of *E. coli*.

13-C To determine whether agent X affects the survival of *E. coli*, an experimenter needs to try different amounts of agent X, keeping temperature, time, and age of *E. coli* constant. If you discovered that fewer bacteria survived when you used more agent X, you could deduce that agent X aids in killing *E. coli*.

14-H 10^2 is the result obtained at 800 minutes in 32°C in Experiment 1 using agent X. If the same result is produced without agent X, then agent X would have no effect on *E. coli*.

15-B Experiments 2 and 3 were about the destruction of bacterial spores, so you need to study Tables 1 and 2. Agent X was not used in either experiment. Knowing this, you could eliminate answer choices **A**, **C**, and **D** because they all include agent X (**I**). All the spores were killed at 130°C in moist heat (Experiment 2) while many were still alive at 130°C in dry heat (Experiment 3). Increased temperature, NOT decreased temperature, killed more spores in both experiments.

16-F For this question you need to examine the choices and see which are true and which are false. In Table 1 you see that at 110°C it took 1 minute to destroy *Bacillus anthracis*. **F** is true. In Table 2, soil spores fared best, so they are NOT relatively vulnerable to dry heat (**G**). No experiment tested the effect of moist heat on vegetative bacteria (**H**). Although some spores in Experiment 3 did survive temperatures at 180°C, we do not know if any would survive at higher than 180°C (**B**) since no higher temperatures were used.

17-C This problem is simple. Experiment 2 involves moist heat. Experiment 3 involves dry heat. *ZAP* **A**, **C**, and **D**. These organisms were in both experiments. Clos. sporogenes were in Experiment 2 only.

Passage IV (Data Representation)

The schematic diagram shows the interaction between four machines: compressor, boiler, turbine, and condenser. Points 1, 2, 3, and 4 are places between each machine where pressure and volume measurements have been taken and are displayed in Graph A. The highest and lowest pressures are recorded as P_1 and P_2. Graph B shows how the difference between the highest and lowest pressure readings affects the efficiency of the work output. The system is most efficient when the amount of work output is closest to the amount of work input.

18-G   The answer is found in Graph A where pressure and volume are plotted. Pressure is shown on the vertical line, where a rising or falling line indicates a change in pressure. Where the graph is horizontal, no change in pressure occurs. There is no change in pressure between points 1 and 4 and points 2 and 3. Looking at the schematic diagram, you see that the boiler and condenser are between these points.

19-C   All answer choices can be found in Graph A, where you will see changes of pressure between points 1 and 2 and points 3 and 4. There is an increase in pressure between 1 and 2 (follow the arrows) and a decrease between 3 and 4. On the schematic diagram the compressor and turbine are between points 1 and 2 and points 3 and 4. Between 3 and 4, work is yielded as the pressure decreases.

20-J   Graph A shows the change in specific volume on the horizontal axis. The greatest jump is between points 1 and 4 which, according to the schematic, is the condenser.

21-A   The question asks about efficiency, which is plotted on the horizontal axis of Graph B. The ratio between two equal values will be 1, so you look for 1 on the horizontal axis to find its corresponding efficiency value. The line shows an efficiency (on the vertical axis) of 0.

22-F   You must understand the meaning of $\frac{P_1}{P_2}$ in the horizontal axis of Graph B. Efficiency increases (as shown by the rising curve) as $P_1 \div P_2$ becomes a greater number. P_1 and P_2 stand for numbers that measure pressure. To raise the value of $P_1 \div P_2$, you need to either increase P_1 or decrease P_2. Only decreasing P_2 is offered as an answer choice.

Science Answer Review
Workout E

Passage I (Data Representation)

1-B   You must look at the chart for River B and decide which one material was in greatest quantity. The graph that occupies the largest area represents the material in greatest quantity. If you counted the rectangles, fine sand covers 19 full rectangles, whereas medium sand occupies 14, and silt, 13.

2-H   For this question you need to examine each answer choice and decide if it is true or false, based on the data. The correct choice will be true. **F** is false. If finer particles were lighter than water, the graphs for these particles would get wider near the top. **G** is false for the same reason. The graphs for coarse and medium sand get wider near the bottom. **C** is true. Clay and silt are the finer particles. Their graphs do not get as wide near the bottom, because they are evenly distributed throughout the depth of the river. **J** is false because the graphs for coarser particles get wider near the bottom.

3-C   Anything that is heavier than water would tend to sink, so the greatest concentrations would be found at the bottom. All the sedimentary materials do this to some degree. Note that if the water weren't moving, all materials would have a chance to sink to the bottom.

4-F   All of the river sediments are heavier than water. This is shown in each graph's tendency to be wider at the bottom. If the sediments were allowed to settle, they would all end up in layers on the bottom.

5-D   Differing turbulence, volume of water, and depth of the river would effect how much each type of material is churned up in the water. However, the *proportion* of materials would be determined by the soil type found on the bottom of each river.

Passage II (Conflicting Viewpoints)

6-H   A careful reading of both viewpoints reveals that both scientists are explaining why the Viking probe recorded no signs of life on Mars. Scientist 1 claims that the probe's search was not thorough; Scientist 2 claims that the probe found no traces of life because there is no life on Mars. Since both scientists are explaining why the Viking probe revealed no signs of life, they agree that no life was found on Mars.

7-B   Scientist 1 argues that Mars is a likely candidate for the existence of life because its "landscape is quite similar to that of the Earth" and has "volcanoes, canyons, and polar ice caps." In citing this as a reason, Scientist 1 is suggesting that similar conditions in the environment could result in similar life forms.

8-F   Scientist 1 insists that further work must be done to find life on Mars. He or she is insisting that it is there and that we haven't found it yet. Scientist 1 is operating on the assumption that life must be there because it is theoretically possible. The fact that life is theoretically possible on Mars is not proof that it actually exists.

9-D   The question is "Would the probe accurately detect life under conditions such as those found on Mars?" To test this, the probe should be tested on a frozen desert region on Earth, where scientists know that it should find some traces of life.

10-H   Scientist 1 argues that Martian life forms may be so different from forms on Earth that it would be difficult to know what to look for. Under these circumstances, Scientist 1 would not support looking for similar life forms.

11-A   The evidence of drastic climatic changes on Mars suggests that if life had developed, it may have been destroyed by one of these drastic changes in climate. Therefore, scientists would be justified in looking for signs of life destroyed by drastically changing climates.

12-F   Neither scientist would say that life forms exist only on Earth. Scientist 1 says "... it seems probable that life does exits there [Mars]." Scientist 2 says, "There may be other forms of life somewhere in the universe ..."

Passage III (Research Summary)

13-C   Only light wavelengths emitted by the gas will get through the two slits and enter the prism. Wavelengths not emitted by the gas will show as black areas on the line spectra.

14-J   In Experiment 2, the dark lines on the line spectra show light wavelengths that were absorbed. Sodium shows more dark lines in the ultraviolet range because it absorbed more ultraviolet light that mercury did.

15-A   According to the line spectra emitted by mercury (Experiment 1), the visible light bands seem concentrated near the blue and green wavelengths. Under these circumstances, it is logical that light emitted from mercury will appear blue and green.

16-H   In the line spectra for Experiment 1, the white bands are wavelengths that are emitted when each of the gases is electrified. In Experiment 2, the black bands are spectra that are absorbed when white light travels through the gases.

The line spectra emitted by mercury shows several bands ranging in size from 250 nm to 700 nm. The line spectra absorbed by mercury shows only one band at about 230 nm. The two spectra have no wavelengths in common, so mercury absorbs none of the spectra that it emits as an electrified gas.

The line spectra emitted by sodium has some lines in common with the line spectra absorbed by sodium. These bands range from 250 nm to 350 nm. Sodium absorbs some but not all of the wavelengths it emits as an electrified gas.

17-D   According to the line spectra of Experiment 2, certain wavelengths of light are absorbed by certain elements. The theory suggests that each wavelength of light corresponds to a certain energy level, so certain elements will absorb light at certain energy levels.

18-G   An application uses the result of an experiment to answer new questions. The result of Experiment I was the discovery of the line spectrum of two gases, mercury and sodium. The only choice that uses this knowledge is **G**. The other choices depend on knowledge that Experiment I *did not* yield, so you can *ZAP* all of them.

Science Answer Review
Workout F

Passage I (Data Representation)

1-B   To answer, you need to compare each answer choice against the graph. **A** is *not* true. The energy increase is shown by the curve that begins at 5 KJ, jumps to 8, then descends to 3. This is not a constant energy increase. **B** *is* true. The intermediate complex is formed at 8 KJ, but has lost 5 KJ by the time it has turned into E + F. **C** is *not* true, because the energy level starts at 5 and ends at 3. **D** is *not* true because the energy level increases by 2 KJ when E + F is changed into A + B.

2-J   The curve in the chart shows the energy level. The far left shows the start of the reaction with an energy level of 5 KJ; the far right shows the end is at 3 KJ which is 2 KJ lower than the beginning.

3-C   The path of the curve is reversible. The forward reaction is from left to right; the reverse, from right to left. In both directions, the reactions begin with an energy gain until they reach 8 KJ, at which point they lose energy.

4-H   If the vertical and horizontal axes remain unchanged, the reverse reaction would be shown as a left/right mirror image of the graph in Figure 1.

5-B   It is important to remember that this question is asking about the reverse reaction. The largest change in energy is a 5 KJ change when E + F change into IC.

Passage II (Research Summary)

6-J   This question tests your knowledge of scientific procedures. The instructor assumed that the rods would expand at a constant rate. You know this because he took only two measurements of the length of the rod—one before and one after heating. Had the instructor not assumed this, he or she would have measured the time and temperature and measured the rod at various points in time as the rod expanded.

7-C   Look at the two charts: both charts show in the last column the total change in length of the rods. In both experiments, the rod that expanded most in Experiment 1 was also the rod that expanded most in Experiment 2. The rods were consistent in their expansion so the projections from the two rods support each other.

8-J   This question tests your knowledge of common safety procedures in a science experiment. Any flammable liquid (which means the same thing as "inflammable liquid") must be safely contained. You need to be familiar with laboratory procedures for the ACT Science Reasoning Test.

9-A   This is a division problem. Look at the bottom row in the chart for Experiment 1. A 100 cm rod expanded .175 cm. If the rod had been 25 cm, or as $\frac{1}{4}$ long, you could figure this out by dividing .175 by 4.

.175 cm ÷ 4 = .04375 cm

Then round .04375 cm up to .044 cm

10-G Anyone familiar with scientific principles could deduce that the expansion of metals is related to molecular activity, but the challenge is to examine the experiment and see if there is anything in the experiment that points to this conclusion. Neither experiment makes a connection between expansion and molecular activity.

11-C This question can be solved empirically. Looking at the net change on both charts, you see that metal X expanded approximately $\frac{3}{5}$ as much as zinc. This means that the coefficient of expansion for metal X would be about $\frac{3}{5}$ of the coefficient of expansion for zinc. Looking at the chart under question 6, you will see that 16.8 (for copper) is about $\frac{3}{5}$ of 26.28 (for zinc).

Passage III (Research Summary)

12-G This question is very *ZAPPABLE*. Each line in the charts of the answer choices represents a column in Table 2. Looking at Table 2 for October, you can see the depth of frozen soil was 1 for each plot. Any correct graph will have all three lines beginning at 1, so you can *ZAP* **F** and **C**. Looking at the data for November, you will see that Plot 1 should be twice the values for Plots 2 and 3. Only **G** shows one line at twice the number as the other two.

13-D In Table 1 you see that the greatest snow cover is in Plot 3, followed by Plot 2, then Plot 1. In Table 1 you see that the depth of frozen ground is greatest in Plot 1, followed by Plot 2, then Plot 3. Where the snow is thickest, the frozen ground is thinnest and vice versa.

14-H One logical conclusion is that the growth of hay would be depressed, as it was for other plants in Plot 1. But since this is not one of the choices, it seems more likely that the effect the activity will have on the hay can not be determined. There is no proof that deep freezing would hinder the growth of hay.

15-A This question requires some insight to scientific procedures. A control needs to resemble the test plot in every way except for the one thing that is being tested. A control plot for a snowmobile-ridden hay field should be an identical hay field without snowmobile traffic.

16-H Plot 1 is the test plot, so the control plot should resemble Plot 1 as closely as possible. Plot 3 is not a very good control plot because it is in the forest, and is quite different from the test plot.

17-D You need to examine each choice to find one that is true. **A** is not true because the experiments do not show that decreased snowcover increased the freezing of plant seeds. **B** is not true because it was not shown that the plot that the snowmobiles tread on experienced a delayed thaw. **C** is not true, because Table 4 shows that Plot 1 never recovered to produce as much vegetation as Plots 2 and 3. **D** is true. Negative correlation means that as one thing increases the other decreases. As the depth of the frozen ground increased, the quantity of vegetation the following summer decreased.

Passage IV (Data Representation)

18-H   It is important to realize that protons and neutrons are expressed as whole numbers, and therefore they can be plotted as exact points on a graph.

19-B   You must look at the graph at the intersection of 40 on the vertical scale and 51 on the horizontal scale. At this intersection is a black square, indicating that a nucleus with 40 protons and 51 neutrons exists and is stable. (Note that the passage describing the graph explains that black points denote stable nuclei.)

20-G   On the graph, a line labeled N = Z shows where nuclei that have equal numbers of protons and neutrons would be plotted. Some with numbers below 10 exist, but as the numbers increase, the graph curves to the right, indicating that the number of neutrons exceeds the number of protons. So the number of protons (Z) divided by the number of neutrons (N) will be less than 1 for most nuclei.

21-C   When a nucleus loses an alpha particle (alpha decay) it loses 2 protons and 2 neutrons. On the chart the new nucleus would be lower and to the left of the old nucleus.

22-F   A scientist is claiming that a stable nucleus (shown in black) can lose a proton without losing a neutron. The chart indicates that this could produce either a stable or unstable nucleus, depending on which nucleus loses the proton. If a stable nucleus loses only a proton, the resulting nucleus would be plotted one number lower on the chart. Some nuclei show unstable nuclei below them (clear); others show stable nuclei (black).

NOTES

NOTES

NOTES

NOTES